Christmas

A CANDID HISTORY

BRUCE DAVID FORBES

UNIVERSITY OF CALIFORNIA PRESS
Berkeley   Los Angeles   London

University of California Press, one of the most
distinguished university presses in the United States,
enriches lives around the world by advancing scholarship
in the humanities, social sciences, and natural sciences.
Its activities are supported by the UC Press Foundation
and by philanthropic contributions from individuals and institutions.
For more information, visit www.ucpress.edu.

Frontispiece: Coca-Cola advertisement. Haddon Sundblom painting, 1953. © CORBIS

UNIVERSITY OF CALIFORNIA PRESS
Berkeley and Los Angeles, California

University of California Press, Ltd.
London, England

Library of Congress Cataloging-in-Publication Data

Forbes, Bruce David.
Christmas : a candid history / Bruce David Forbes.
p.   cm.
Includes bibliographical references and index.
ISBN-13: 978-0-520-25104-5 (cloth : alk. paper)
1. Christmas—History.   I. Title.

GT4985.F67 2007
394.2663—dc22
2007000366

Manufactured in the United States of America

16   15   14   13   12   11   10   09   08   07
    10   9   8   7   6   5   4   3   2   1

This book is printed on New Leaf EcoBook 50, a 100% recycled fiber of which 50% is de-inked
post-consumer waste, processed chlorine-free. EcoBook 50 is acid-free and meets the minimum
requirements of ANSI/ASTM D5634–01 (*Permanence of Paper*).

CONTENTS

Illustrations follow Chapter Four

ACKNOWLEDGMENTS

I am overwhelmed by the interest, support, and assistance offered by so many colleagues, family members, and friends as I have worked on this project, and no words of gratitude say enough. I want to thank editor Reed Malcolm in particular, for his guidance, his patience, and his enthusiastic interest in the book from the very beginning. Gene Gallagher also has been especially helpful, with specific suggestions and supportive friendship. Morningside College President John Reynders and Dean William Deeds granted me a sabbatical during which I was able to write most of this book. Many others have assisted me in so many ways: Calvin Roetzel, Robert Jewett, Mark Reasoner, Philip Anderson, Ann Pflaum, Dell deChant, Randy Maddox, Ted Campbell, Mark Seeley, Ann-Marie Andreasson-Hogg, Jim Fisk, Kate Warne, Edith Gladstone, Stephen Leida, Jan Carrier, Kimberly Nelson-Finch, Linda Miller, Corinne Schuster, Rusty Brace, Tammy Huf, Melissa Dreyer, and Stacey Baldus. One person who makes all of these efforts worthwhile is my son Matthew, a great dialogue partner of whom I am so proud.

INTRODUCTION

I love Christmas. And Christmas drives me crazy.

Based upon reactions from family, friends, and colleagues, I am not alone in both responses to the Christmas season. On one hand, I love the music, lights, and family gatherings, along with the story of the Christ child, shepherds, and wise men, and the messages of generosity, love, joy, and peace. On the other hand, I am frustrated by how hectic and commercialized the season has become, and worried that all of the cultural trappings can overwhelm spiritual aspects of Christmas. At times the reality of my Christmas experiences fails to live up to my idealized expectations. In addition, I have questions about the impact that this culturally dominant holiday has upon my friends who are Jewish, or Muslim, or secular. So Christmas is my favorite season of the year, but it is also a very mixed bag.

After wrestling with various reactions to Christmas, I decided to find out how Christmas got to be the way it is today. Tracing the history of this annual celebration has changed the way I look at many Christmas-related issues. And once I started down that road, seeking a brief, candid history of Christmas, curiosity took over. Simple curiosity may be the best motivation for learning about all kinds of things, because it helps us avoid being captured by heavy-handed agendas from whatever direction. Part of the fascination comes when we encounter surprises along the way, commenting to ourselves, "I didn't know that." Here are several interesting examples.

- early Christians in the first two or three centuries did not celebrate Christmas
- Puritans in England and in New England made Christmas observances illegal
- Saint Nicholas is an *elf* in the famous poem "The Night Before Christmas"
- the United States Congress regularly met on Christmas Day into the 1850s
- President Franklin Roosevelt changed the date of Thanksgiving in order to lengthen the Christmas shopping season

This book seeks to provide a brief, candid history of Christmas, for general audiences, for people who, like me, wonder how the Christmas celebration got to be the way it is. The word "candid" highlights one of my intentions. Many acquaintances have told me they want to hear the "real" story of Christmas, something more than sugar-coated or romanticized versions. And when I hear explanations of certain Christmas traditions, I too think, is this just a great story that tugs at my heart strings, or is it also historical? How did it really happen? Do we even know?

To find some answers, it seems sensible to consult the good academic Christmas books available these days, books I really appreciate. But many are long, or technical and full of jargon, and usually specialized. Several books focus on the American Christmas but say very little about earlier developments, and other books concentrate only on the first few centuries, or on Saint Nicholas, or on Christmas carols. One friend told me he was interested in an overall story of how Christmas developed, but not a 400-page volume or, even worse, a list of ten books. As he remarked, "I'm curious, not obsessed."

I have written this little volume in an attempt to answer that request. I claim no major new breakthrough thesis. Much of the content of this book is a distillation of information scattered throughout many books, although I also have consulted some of the original sources myself. My contributions may come in analogies and examples, and in the way I structure the overview to try to make sense of it all.

For several years I have given short presentations on the history of Christmas, and audiences tend to offer two responses. First, they comment that they knew some of the information and tidbits, simply from newspaper articles or television programs in the Christmas season, but that many other details came as a surprise. The surprise varies from person to person. Second, they say that the presentation helped them put the miscellaneous details together into an overall picture of how Christmas developed. There is no shortage of Christmas information out there. For example, at least two excellent, reliable Christmas encyclopedias are available, and some other books answer Christmas questions in short little chunks, a page or two at a time. As I tie the pieces together, I often leave out exceptions and variations. Keeping in mind the danger of oversimplifying, I hope the broad overview will be helpful.

The opening chapter, "First There Was Winter," argues that many of our favorite aspects of the Christmas season, such as lights and evergreen decorations, are predictable features of midwinter festivals that existed long before Christianity. This is what people are referring to when they talk about the "pagan" roots of Christmas traditions. My emphasis is simply to recognize that a midwinter carnival is a very understandable way for human beings to cope with winter, and yes, the widespread human impulse to party in the face of winter has influenced the development of Christmas, then and now.

"Christmas Comes Late," the second chapter, explains why the Christian church did not celebrate the birth of Jesus in its earliest years. Two or three centuries passed before Christians created Epiphany observances or selected December 25 as Jesus' birthday. In fact, Christian scriptures say very little about the birth of the Christ child, and over time Christians have had to fill in the story with many additional, beloved traditions.

Christmas became a major Christian celebration at the same time that Christianity began to spread from the Mediterranean region into central and northern Europe, and when it did, Christianity picked up aspects of various European winter festivals. The title of the third chapter provides an image that summarizes the process, at least for me: "Christmas Is Like a Snowball." Christmas rolled through Europe, and later into the Americas and elsewhere, picking up some features and dropping others, with the Christmas tree as one example. Though Puritans in England and America tried to suppress Christmas, the influence of people like Charles Dickens, Queen Victoria, and Prince Albert eventually revived it, but in an altered form.

The fourth chapter offers a case study of the snowball process, the fascinating story of how Saint Nicholas traditions arose, spread throughout Europe, eventually morphed into Santa Claus in the United States, and then found their way to other parts of the world. The process involved a significant shift from a legendary bishop and saint (Nicholas) to a jolly gift giver (Santa Claus), which leads to the topic of the next chapter, "And Then There Was Money." For most of us, the commercialization of Christmas refers to an overwhelming preoccupation with gifts. The fifth chapter explains that the emphasis on gifts is recent, arising especially in the last three centuries. Yet it is about more than gifts. The business possibilities of Christmas have extended to many other products as well: Christmas cards, wrapping paper, decorations, movies, and even music.

Following this historical overview, the final chapter discusses some of the personal issues the holiday season raises. One of my professors in graduate school said that history involved two questions: What? and So What? My comments in "Wrestling with Christmas" are only a beginning, but I believe it is worthwhile to reflect on the implications of this historical summary for our own holiday celebrations.

Along the way throughout the book, in an attempt to tell the "real" story, I occasionally refer to topics where scholars disagree. I try not to get too mired in the technicalities, and sometimes I offer no solutions, but I want to alert readers to subject areas where questions have been raised. I use backnotes sparingly, but they are included, to give proper credit for quotations and to point interested readers to further sources. I also try to say some things plainly, when other academic discussions may delicately allude to them.

Even though I have written this book to satisfy the curiosity of those who would like to read a brief, accessible overview, I hope that many readers will become so fascinated that they just *have* to read more. Thus for each source in the bibliography I include the page count and the presence or absence of notes, bibliography, and index. Each entry has annotations on the author's perspective, the book's subject matter, and sometimes its level of difficulty. I trust this will be a genuinely useful list for those who want to learn more.

Finally, a note about the word *Christmas:* In the English-speaking world it began as "Christ's Mass," referring to a special midnight mass, the worship service that marked the beginning of Christmas Day. The word *Christmas* dates back perhaps as far as the eleventh century. As we English-speaking people have come to employ the term it is a little confusing, when you think about it, because we use it in at least two different ways. Sometimes when we speak of Christmas, we are referring to the story of Jesus' birth and the various events surrounding it. That, we often say, was the real Christmas or the first Christmas. According to this usage or definition, when I say that "I want to learn about Christmas," what I mean is that I would like to know more about the details of when, where, and how Jesus was born, and what it means. At other times we refer not to the events surrounding Jesus' birth but to the annual celebration of his birth. For instance, when we talk about Christmas in medieval Europe, or when we complain about what Christmas has become, we are using the term in this second sense. So sometimes we use the term *Christmas* to refer to the events surrounding Jesus' birth, and sometimes we use it to refer to the later annual celebrations.

During the Christmas season when I began to write this book, two American commercial television networks aired specials about the history of Christmas. I watched each one, and what I expected was an account of the way Christmas celebrations have changed over the years, because I had the second definition of Christmas in mind. Instead, both television specials dealt with the question of how much of the nativity story was literally true. They interviewed scholars with contrasting views, and it was all very interesting, but they were using the other definition, focusing on the story of Jesus' birth.

The fact is that the general public, including me, uses the term *Christmas* in *both* ways, and that is likely to continue. When I use the word in this book, I have tried to assure that the context makes clear which sense I have in mind.

one

———◆———

FIRST THERE
WAS WINTER

To understand what Christmas has become, first we should consider winter.

For the moment, set aside everything you have heard about the baby Jesus in a manger, and shepherds and wise men, and think instead about winter. Of course, the characteristics of winter vary with location because, depending upon where you live, winter is a more dramatic reality for some people than for others. I assume that most readers of this book are North American, and thus I will emphasize the Northern Hemisphere, but an emphasis on the Northern Hemisphere also reflects the early and medieval history of Christianity. The Christian church was born in the Mediterranean region, but within a few centuries its headquarters became centered in Rome and Constantinople, a northward shift from its Jerusalem beginnings. Then Christianity began to spread throughout Europe, and the further north it moved, the more winter became a factor.

So, what is winter like? The answer is not difficult: basically, it is cold and it is dark. The further north you move, the rain turns to sleet and snow, and the temperatures drop low enough to discourage much of the outdoor work and play that human beings enjoy the rest of the year. And the days are shorter, with so many more hours of darkness.

Several years ago I led a group of college students on a May interim trip to Alaska, and my experience there caused me to think a lot about winter. We were based in the little village of Willow, Alaska, about an hour and a half's drive north of Anchorage, still in the southern half of that enormous state. May is a beautiful time in Alaska, essentially spring, when both leaves and tourists begin to appear. What caused me to think about winter was a conversation with the minister of a little mission church in Willow who mentioned that he brought seminary interns to Alaska not in May but in January, when they could work with people who were in the midst of their greatest struggles. He said that the temperatures could get down to 50 degrees below zero, *before* calculating wind chill, with little more than five hours of daylight per day. That is the season of the year in Alaska when depression settles in, when alcoholism and other forms of chemical dependency are at their worst, and when incidents of domestic violence soar. That, he said, is when people really need help.

My imagination began to wander to people in the medieval and Renaissance-Reformation eras in central and northern Europe. Without the modern conveniences I take for granted, what must it have been like for them to keep their homes warm, or to get work done, or simply to cope with so much darkness? Even now, when we have thermostats and electric lights, we still talk about seasonal affective disorder and cabin fever, indications of our continuing battle with winter.

Especially in northern regions, winter remains a challenge for human beings to survive. In a way, the approach of winter is a little like walking into death, hoping we will emerge on the other side. The natural world accents that feeling, as the trees and other plants appear to die, and animals hibernate, and blizzards threaten. Survivors look forward to the new life and exhilaration that spring will bring.

Even before studying the history and anthropology of early cultures, we could guess what human beings might do to cope with these realities of winter. A great idea would be to organize a big, blowout, midwinter party. It would be perfect. People could have something to look forward to for the first half of winter, the preparations could be a welcome distraction, and the party itself would be a blast. Then, once it was over, the remainder of winter would be that much shorter, until spring finally brought liberation from the cold and darkness.

Also, again before studying early cultures, we could guess what the party would be like. When should it happen? The ideal time would be when the days stop getting shorter and are poised to begin lengthening again, in mid to late December. And we can guess other features of the party. First of all, it would have to be a festival of lights, pushing back the oppressive darkness, featuring candles and torches and burning logs. It would also make sense to highlight evergreens as symbols or decorations, because the greenery could serve as signs of life in the midst of apparent death. We might look for other plants that stay green and, against the norm, even bear fruit in the middle of winter, like holly, or mistletoe. Of course, there would be feasting and drinking, probably to excess, as there is at almost any party. Obviously, a midwinter celebration would involve gatherings of people, perhaps the whole village, or selected neighbors, friends, and family; an individual might sponsor or attend several such gatherings throughout the festivity period. As the midwinter festivities go on year after year, special music would undoubtedly develop for the season. And, of course, many parties involve gifts.

All of this is not just speculation. This kind of midwinter celebration is indeed what human beings did throughout Europe, in many different cultures, before Christianity, and we will look at two specific examples in a moment. Mulling over the commonsense appeal of midwinter celebrations, as sketched out here, many persons today are surprised to realize that much of what they love about the Christmas season is not really Christmas at all. We love the lights, the evergreen decorations, the music and the food, the chance to get together with family and friends, and the special feeling of warmth that comes with the festivities. Yet all of these features have no necessary connection with a story of a baby Jesus in a manger. Instead they are the predictable characteristics of midwinter festivities.

This is what it means when some people say that Christmas has pagan roots. In essence, "pagan" is a word that means non-Christian, or in this case, pre-Christian. And yes, it is true that midwinter celebrations existed throughout Europe before Jesus was born and before the Christian religion developed. Seeing a contest between "pagan" religions and Christianity, some Christians try to protect themselves from any association with rival religions. Another way to view it is that a midwinter celebration is simply an understandable human impulse, to help people survive winter. If a culture did not already have such a celebration, people would make one up. Participating in a midwinter festival is an indication of our common humanity, across many cultures and many religions. It just makes sense, as a human coping mechanism.

What are some actual examples of such pre-Christian winter festivals? The evidence is often limited, so we cannot describe them in the kind of detail that is possible for more recent times. Three general points should be kept in mind.

First, because of variations in climate, agricultural patterns, and changing calendars, the winter festivals were not all in mid-December but tended to occur more broadly over two months or so, from what we now call November into the early days of January. Influenced by the Roman calendar, we now celebrate the "new year" on January 1, but there were many possible occasions to mark a new year: when the harvest was in and farmers had leisure to look ahead (November), or at the winter solstice, when daylight once again begins to lengthen (December), or at the beginning of the Roman annual calendar, which falls only a few days after the winter solstice (January). As cultures interacted with one another, some of the customs of these various winter festivals migrated back and forth across a two to three month period.

Second, the further back we go, the fewer documents we have to provide a description of the customs of a people. We then have to draw conclusions from physical artifacts, or we "reconstruct" festivals "from survivals in popular custom."[1] That simply means that we examine some of the customs in more recent times and speculate about how long they have existed and how they might have started. Yet, although we may be uncertain about some of the details, and scholars may argue and revise specific theories, the general features of midwinter festivities we have just summarized arise again and again.

Third, the character of the winter celebrations was shaped not just by changing weather alone but also by winter's impact on the lifestyle of agricultural people, in preindustrial societies. Late fall and early winter brought the harvest of crops and also the slaughter of some livestock, so that there would be fewer animals to feed throughout the winter. With no freezers available, some meat might be stored for a while in the season's cold temperatures, and other meat would be salted for preservation. Most people would prefer to eat the fresh meat right away, when it tasted best. In addition, alcohol could be fermented from the recently harvested crops. These agricultural realities all created the perfect combination for exuberant parties in winter: leisure, fresh meat, harvested crops, and alcohol.[2]

𝕭 SATURNALIA AND YULE 𝕭

Two examples of the resulting winter festivals are the Saturnalia of ancient Rome, and Yule or Jul in northern Europe. Both illustrate the common features that we speculated would be part of winter parties, and both influenced Christmas when Christianity spread into Europe.

Saturnalia began in Rome at least two hundred years before the lifetime of Jesus, apparently arising out of some kind of agricultural harvest festival. Theories vary about the origins of the Roman god Saturn, but by the era of Christianity he was viewed as an agricultural god who, in an earlier golden age, had established a village on the Capitoline Hill, one of the seven hills of Rome. Legends said that he had taught people how to till the soil and had presided over an era of prosperity, peace, and happiness. Every December 17 a sacrifice was offered to Saturn in the Roman Forum, but what mattered most to the general public was the feasting and partying that followed, varying from three to seven days, until December 23. Hence Saturnalia is sometimes a singular term, referring to the overall celebration, or a plural term, referring to the several days.

In the words of the *Oxford Classical Dictionary,* "The Saturnalia were the merriest festival of the year, 'the best of days.'"[3] No one worked during this period, except those whose help was needed to provide food for the lavish feasts. Friends visited each other from home to home and also joined in boisterous street processions. Houses, great halls, and streets were decorated with laurel, green trees, and shrubs, illuminated by candles and lamps. Major bonfires were lit at high ground where many citizens could see them. People exchanged small gifts, such as wax candles, wax fruit, and clay dolls.

The two major themes of the idealized Saturnalian golden age were abundance and equality. "In this era of joy and plenty, people lived together in harmony and shared equally in the earth's bounty."[4] In real life, people of Rome were treated very differently, depending on whether they were part of the nobility, or artisans, or slaves, but in the few days of the annual Saturnalia celebration everyone was to be treated equally. Lucian of Samosota (about 120–180), a Greek commentator on Roman culture and society, wrote a dialogue between Saturn (also called Cronus) and his priest, and the conversation included rules of the Saturnalia. During the celebration, Saturn proclaimed, "Let every man be treated equal, slave and freeman, poor and rich," and he also directed that "no one may be ill-tempered or cross or threaten anybody." When it came to banquets, the guidelines included:

> Each man shall take the couch where he happens to be. Rank, family, or wealth shall have little influence on privilege [that is, on a man's place at table].

All shall drink the same wine, and neither stomach trouble nor headache shall give the rich man an excuse for being the only one to drink the better quality.

All shall have their meat on equal terms. The waiters shall not show favor to anyone. . . . Neither are large portions to be placed before one and tiny ones before another, nor a ham for one and a pig's jaw for another—all must be treated equally. . . .

When a rich man gives a banquet to his servants, his friends shall aid him in waiting on them.[5]

The last instruction especially refers to a practice of social inversion, or a reversal of roles. Not only were slaves excused from their duties and not subject to punishments during the Saturnalia, but masters sometimes waited on slaves at banquets.

Even more, a Mock King would be chosen by lot to preside over the Saturnalia, which meant that a person of any social standing had a chance to become the temporary king. In Lucian's dialogue, Saturn said to his priest that if he became king "you not only escape silly orders but can give them yourself, telling one man to shout out something disgraceful about himself, another to dance naked, pick up the flute-girl, and carry her three times around the house."[6] Later Christmas practices in medieval Europe included similar customs that temporarily elevated average people, although it is unclear if they derived directly from the Mock Kings of the Roman Saturnalia. In communities of medieval France, Switzerland, and other areas a boy was chosen as "bishop for a day" on Holy Innocents' Day, December 28, when Christians remembered Herod's massacre of children. In late medieval and Renaissance England, some towns chose a "lord of misrule" as a sort of jester to preside over merrymaking in the Christmas season. On the eve of Epiphany (to be explained in the next chapter), many European cultures dropped a bean, a coin, or some other token into a cake or pudding, and whoever found the bean in his or her piece of cake would be anointed

King of the Bean, or Queen of the Bean. All of these practices seem remarkably similar to the earlier Mock Kings of the Roman Saturnalia.

As some descriptions have hinted already, the Saturnalia gained a reputation for wanton behavior, with excessive drinking, gambling, and other unrestrained activities. Again in Lucian's dialogue, Saturn said that in his festive time he could "drink and be drunk, shout, play games and dice, appointing masters of the revels, feast the servants, sing stark naked, clap and shake, and sometimes even get pushed head-first into cold water with my face smeared with soot."[7] Clearly he was describing the behavior of the crowds, not himself alone. If you look up "saturnalia" in an English-language dictionary today, one of the definitions will be something like "an unrestrained often licentious celebration: orgy," associated with excess and extravagance.[8]

Thus, the Roman Saturnalia serves as the first example of a winter festival that existed prior to Christianity, and it fits many of our general expectations: light from candles and fires, greenery, feasting, gifts, and social gatherings, all in mid-December. In addition, the Saturnalia included customs of social inversion that might not always be expected in winter festivals, but they set a precedent whose echoes arose later in European Christmas celebrations.

A second example is Yule, or Jul, the Scandinavian equivalent, in northern Europe. Geographically it involves the Teutonic peoples in what we now call northern Germany, Scandinavia, and the British Isles. Here our information about pre-Christian practices is especially sketchy, because in some regions Christian missionaries were busy transcribing the native languages as best they could, thus introducing literacy. In those situations, all of the written records would be post-Christian and thus potentially influenced by Christianity. To describe cultural practices before the introduction of Christianity, scholars have built theories on the basis of artifacts and surviving customs (and, as I said before, guesswork).

These days, people assume that Yule or Jul is simply another name for Christmas, and many dictionaries define the terms that way: "the feast of the nativity of Jesus Christ."[9] However, the terms Yule and Jul clearly existed in the region before Christianity arrived, associated with winter activities of some sort, although scholars are not exactly sure what the words meant. One theory argues for "wheel," referring to the cycle of the year, and another theory claims "sacrifice" or "feast," referring to religious animal sacrifices and/or winter banquets and celebrations. Only later did the words Yule or Jul become associated with Christmas, the imported winter festival.

Turning to Old Norse customs as an example of northern European practices, we find Jul festivities in early winter, at the conclusion of the slaughter of livestock and the brewing of ale, with the feasting and drinking that would naturally follow. The celebrations were probably mixed with animal sacrifices and other religious observances to encourage fertility in the coming year. One piece of evidence comes from the writings of historian Snorri Sturluson (1179–1241), whose *Heimskringla* told the story of Norway's early kings, based upon poetry that had been passed on through oral tradition. He wrote, "It was ancient custom that when sacrifice was made all farmers were to come to the temple and bring along with them the food they needed while the feast lasted. At this feast all were to take part in the drinking of ale. Also all kinds of livestock were killed in connection with it."[10] As additional evidence, the oldest Christian laws enacted in Norway included a ban on animal sacrifice, which suggests that animal sacrifice was a common Viking practice prior to Christianity.

With a number of varying theories from scholars, "what most researchers do agree upon is that ritual beer drinking featured prominently" in the Viking festivities. When Snorri Sturluson quoted a poem about Harald Fairhair, the king who united Norway into a single realm, two key words state that Harald intended to "drink jul" even when he was away from Norway. It is an interesting phrase. If someone said they were going to "drink Christmas," we would assume that drinking was a key part of their celebration, and we can assume the same thing in the case of the Viking Jul. The drinking may even have had religious connections. Kathleen

Stokker, an American scholar of Norwegian folklore and language, reports a belief that "the celebrants who ritually passed the drinking horn from mouth to mouth sought an ecstatic connection with each other and with the gods."[11]

It is likely that the Viking Jul also involved ancestor worship, beliefs about the return of the dead, and ghost stories. To understand a possible connection, imagine yourself huddled in a cabin in the far north as a blizzard rages outside, accompanied by howling winds and strange sounds. It might seem as if creatures or spirits were riding across the sky. Folklore from many areas of Europe provided different stories that would explain the sounds, in what became known as the wild hunt, *Asgardsreid* (Asgard's ride), Gabriel's hounds, and other names. In Norway it was the *Gandreid*, or spirits' ride, in which spirits of those who had died in the preceding year, an army of the dead, roared through the night. In many cases in northern Europe the wild hunt was led by Odin (Wotan in Germany), a somewhat frightening one-eyed god, with white hair and a beard, who rode a flying eight-legged horse. In the last century scholars have argued that beliefs about the wild hunt were so similar throughout northern Europe that they must have resulted, not simply from frightening winter weather, but also from the spread of secret religious societies centered on the mythology of Odin. This attention to the spirits of the dead also made Jul a natural time for ghost stories, a common practice in the season of the year that was dominated by darkness and leisure. It makes me think of camping as a child, sitting around a fire at night and telling scary stories. Viking winter oral traditions contain just such tales. (At a later time in England, even Charles Dickens's *Christmas Carol* is essentially a ghost story.)

One further feature of the Jul observances was fire. Bonfires and candles not only brought light but were also believed to keep evil spirits away, or to warm the spirits of the dead. Best known today is the Yule Log, a practice that probably predated the introduction of Christianity. Families and communities selected huge logs that could burn in a fireplace for days, and charred remains of the previous year's log were used to ignite the new one. In addition, evergreen branches may have been hung on doorposts and around windows, in the hope that their prickly needles also would ward off evil spirits.

So this was Yule or Jul. E. O. James, a scholar of seasonal celebrations, summarized Yule this way: as winter began and cattle were slaughtered in northern Europe, "a great banquet was held on the fresh meat, accompanied with fire rites and the usual expressions of autumnal rejoicings, coupled with the placation of the dead and the ancestral spirits."[12] And yes, ritual drinking was included. As in the case of the Saturnalia, once again we notice predictable features of winter parties, including light, greenery, feasts, and social gatherings.

When a birthday celebration for Jesus finally got started and then moved into Europe, it encountered and eventually mingled with already well-established traditions like the Saturnalia and Yule. Keep all of this in mind as background to understand the development of Christmas.

two

CHRISTMAS
COMES LATE

☙ THE EARLIEST CENTURIES ❧

Early Christians had no Christmas. The first written evidence of an annual celebration on December 25 commemorating the birth of Jesus comes from the fourth century. Epiphany developed a little earlier, in the eastern portion of the Christian church, but it was not quite the same as what we now call Christmas. Compared with many other aspects of early Christianity, Christmas was a later development.

This comes as a surprise for many of us, because we usually think of Christmas and Easter as the two most special times of the Christian year. It was not always that way. Early Christianity was, instead, an Easter-centered religion. The death and resurrection of Jesus were the center of the early Christian message. An expectation that Jesus would return soon, at any time, and the examples of Christians who endured martyrdom rather than honor Roman gods, caused early Christians to focus on death and resurrection themes. As an illustration, when martyrs and saints became recognized within the church, Christians noted the dates of their death, not of their birth. In a sense, the death dates had become their real birthdays, into eternal life.

Origen, a prolific and influential early Christian writer (approximately 185–254), had some particularly interesting views about birthdays. He noted that both Pharaoh and Herod had birthday celebrations, according to biblical accounts, but each of them had "stained the festival of his birth by shedding human blood." Pharaoh, on his birthday, had ordered the killing of his chief baker (Genesis 40:20–22), and Herod had agreed to behead John the Baptist (Mark 6:14–29, Matthew 14:1–12, Luke 9:7–9). Origen concluded that "not one from all the saints is found to have celebrated a festive day or a great feast on the day of his birth. No one is found to have had joy on the day of the birth of his son or daughter. Only sinners rejoice over this kind of birthday." Further, he wrote that saints "not only do not celebrate a festival on their birth days, but, filled with the Holy Spirit, they curse that day." He referred to Jeremiah ("Cursed be the day on which I was born," Jeremiah 20:14), as well as similar statements attributed to Job and David (Job 3:3–6 and Psalm 51:5). The whole discussion communicates a general attitude held by some early Christians that birthdays were something that only "pagans" (non-Christians) celebrated, not good Christians. "The worthless man who loves things connected with birth keeps birthday festivals," Origen wrote.[1] With that attitude, birthday celebrations, even Jesus' birthday, would not be high on the priority list of early Christians.

In fact, if you think about it, the Christian New Testament says surprisingly little about Jesus' birth. It is generally acknowledged that, of the various books eventually included in the New Testament, Paul's letters were written earliest, and those letters say nothing specific about the birth of Jesus.[2] Perhaps Paul knew nothing about a nativity story of Jesus, or perhaps he did not consider it important.

Among the various New Testament books, the four gospels tell us the most about the life story of Jesus. Christians disagree about whether the gospels were actually written by Matthew, Mark, Luke, or John, or by authors representing traditions associated with those people, but for convenience I will use the personal names. What is important here is that only two of the four gospels include a nativity account. The gospel of Mark, the one that most scholars say was the first of the four gospels to be written, begins in the very first chapter with John the Baptist and John's baptism of Jesus, who by that time was already an adult. In other words, Mark's gospel totally skips the birth of Jesus. The gospel of John, which is different in many ways from the other three gospels, begins with some famous, flowery words: "In the beginning was the Word, and the Word was with God, and the Word was God." A few verses later John writes, "And the Word became flesh and lived among us, and we have seen his glory, the glory as of a father's only son, full of grace and truth" (John 1:14). Of course, Christians eventually applied those two verses to the nativity story, but there is nothing else about Jesus' birth in the gospel of John. John tells us nothing about a baby lying in a manger, no wise men or shepherds, no birth story.

That leaves us with two gospels, Matthew and Luke, and they do provide nativity stories, but they are quite different from each other. In Matthew, an angel announces to Joseph the forthcoming birth of Jesus, and Matthew's narrative also includes wise men, the moving star, and the family's escape to Egypt to avoid Herod's persecution. None of that is in Luke's gospel. Instead, Luke tells of an angel appearing to Mary rather than to Joseph, and the gospel of Luke is the one that includes shepherds and a multitude of angels appearing to them in the fields. None of that is in Matthew's gospel. The two gospels agree on a few basic things, such as the names of Jesus' parents and Mary's virginity. Overall, each gospel provides only a minimal account of the birth of Jesus, with different details. When Christians eventually got around to organizing a special annual celebration of the birth of Jesus, they had to take the few crumbs provided by Matthew and Luke, put them together, and then add some additional traditions, in order to get much of a story to work with.

If you examine the rest of the Christian New Testament, there is nothing more to amplify the birth story of Jesus. Out of twenty-seven total books in the New Testament, only two tell about Jesus' nativity, and their accounts are quite brief. The overall point is that, for the early Christians, the Christmas story was not a primary focus, and the Christian scriptures are evidence of that.

By the way, one other factor also discouraged an observance of the birth of Jesus. In order to have a birthday party for someone, it helps to know the day on which the person was born. In this case a huge problem looms, because nothing in the New Testament indicates the month or the day of Jesus' birth, and there is even some uncertainty about the exact year. Putting questions about the year aside for a moment, consider first the issue of the month and day. The gospels of Matthew and Luke provide no direct indication of a date for the birth of Jesus, and scholars have found no external forms of evidence, and no other traditions, to solve the mystery. In the second and third centuries some Christians tried to determine the date of Jesus' birth, but their conclusions varied widely. One hint that people often seized upon was that Luke's gospel said the shepherds "were living in the field, keeping watch over their flock by night" (Luke 2:8). Does that point at least to a general season of the year and thus help narrow things down? Perhaps, but not much, because shepherds in the region tended their flocks outside for at least three seasons of the year, excluding only winter. With a variety of arguments to support their views, assorted Christians in the second, third, and fourth centuries argued for March 25 and 28, April 19 and 20, May 20, and November 18 as the birth date. If we ask about the specific day on which Jesus was born, the honest answer is that we simply do not know.[3]

I mentioned that there are even questions about the year. Most of us assume that Jesus was born in the year 1, with Jesus' birth as the dividing line between BC and AD. That calendar system for numbering the years, which has become a dominant system in many parts of the world, was developed by a monk approximately five hundred years after the lifetime of Jesus. The monk, Dionysius Exiguus, or Dionysius the Short, intended to create a calendar that would place Jesus at the center. But he made a mistake in his calculations, because we now have evidence that Herod died in the year we label 4 BC. If the gospels of Matthew and Luke are correct in asserting that Jesus was born in the time of Herod, the birthday of Jesus would have to be earlier, and most scholars suggest somewhere between 6 and 4 BC.

So, besides the minimal attention given to Jesus' nativity by the early church, one more reason that the early Christians did not celebrate the birth of Jesus is that they did not know the date on which it had occurred. That of course raises the question of why most Christians now celebrate the birth of Jesus on December 25, and we will get to that shortly.

⚓ EPIPHANY ⚓

In western Christianity we have no clear evidence for an annual celebration focused on the birth of Jesus until the fourth century, but one other related Christian observance, Epiphany, arose somewhat earlier among eastern Christians. I will make several references to "eastern Christianity" and "western Christianity," so let me briefly explain this division for those who are not familiar with the background. Jesus, and the religion of Christianity, were born into the Roman Empire, a vast realm that extended around the Mediterranean Sea. This empire had an important cultural division within it, generally summarized as Greek and Latin. When many of us took a basic Western civilization history course in high school or college, we learned first about ancient Greek civilization, including Socrates, democracy, the Olympic Games, and so many other Greek contributions, and then we learned about Roman civilization that arose later and conquered Greek areas plus additional territory. Yet the Greek side of the empire did not feel fully conquered, often seeing itself as culturally superior and only tolerating the control exerted by Roman military might. The Greek portion of the empire was the eastern side of the Mediterranean, extending from Egypt through Palestine up to what we now call Syria, Turkey, and Greece. The western side, using Latin as a common language, encompassed both northern Africa and southern Europe, including Italy. With this kind of unofficial fault line, there was a cultural fissure running through the Roman Empire, creating east-west, or Greek-Latin, differences. It should come as no surprise that, when Christianity spread throughout the Mediterranean, Christianity also developed cultural divisions similar to the larger cultural tensions in the empire, with Greek-speaking and Latin-speaking Christians, and with contrasting practices and theological tendencies. We might picture Christianity in its first thousand years as a rope with two strands, east and west, wound together. They were unified as one church, more or less, but the two strands kept pulling apart, and by the eleventh century they came unraveled. Today's heirs of the eastern side are Orthodox Christians, and the heirs of the western side are both Roman Catholics and Protestants.

The earliest celebrations of Epiphany arose in eastern Christianity, although even that claim is debated by a few scholars. The fact is, our knowledge about the earliest forms of Epiphany is very sketchy. The noted historian Roland Bainton began a classic article on the topic by stating simply, "The origins of the Christian feast of Epiphany on the sixth of January are still obscure," and unfortunately, very little has been clarified in the years since he wrote those words.[4] This is frustrating when we try to summarize the origins not only of Epiphany but also of Christmas, because our evidence is so fragmentary. Even when we are fortunate to have some documents, we are often forced to rely on copies made centuries later, and that naturally leads to additional questions about the authenticity of the copies. So the most candid answer to many of our questions is "we do not know," and even though scholars frequently seem very certain of themselves in their vigorous academic debates, our theories about the earliest beginnings of Epiphany and Christmas are educated guesses. It also means that almost any generalization I offer probably has some scholar, somewhere, who would dissent.

"Epiphany" comes from a Greek word meaning "manifestation" or "showing forth," and in this context it refers to how Jesus was revealed or made manifest to the world as the son of God. Thinking about the different ways that Christians believe Jesus Christ was disclosed to the world, we can imagine a number of biblical stories that Christians might feature in an "epiphany" celebration or feast. One obvious candidate for emphasis would be the baptism of Jesus, because that is when some gospels say that a dove (or the Holy Spirit, like a dove) descended on Jesus and a voice proclaimed Jesus to be God's son. With dramatic signs like that, certainly Jesus' baptism would be considered an epiphany, showing forth who Jesus was. Another event we might emphasize is the miracle when Jesus turned water into wine at a wedding in Cana, because that was the first of Jesus' public miracles, at least according to the gospel of John. We could also add other miracles, especially very public ones, like Jesus feeding the five thousand. In addition, it certainly would make sense to bring up the birth of Jesus, appearing into the world accompanied by signs and wonders. Yet part of the message of the nativity stories is that the world tended to ignore this baby rather than recognize his importance, so it might not be the best emphasis for an Epiphany celebration. Perhaps a better focus would be the appearance of the magi or wise men, because bringing their gifts to the Christ child could symbolize the world's recognition of Jesus. I have described these possibilities as speculation, but in fact, all of these themes have been included in Epiphany celebrations at one time or another, in varying mixtures, at various places: Jesus' baptism, certain miracles, his birth, and the wise men. Epiphany has always had a very mixed focus.

The earliest indication of what might be called Epiphany festivities comes in comments by Clement of Alexandria (approximately 150–215), who mentioned that the "followers of Basilides" in Egypt celebrated Jesus' *baptism* on January 6. This group, although they saw themselves as Christians, were eventually considered heretics by the majority church. We do not know if other Christians in that region also had such observances, in the same years or shortly thereafter. Maybe, maybe not. A prevailing view is that, although we cannot chart exactly how or when, Epiphany spread throughout the eastern portion of the Christian church and, by sometime in the 300s,

Epiphany on January 6 had become a widely observed day among eastern Christians. By then it also appears that Epiphany had become more focused on the nativity, although still mixed with other themes. When Roman (western) Christians eventually started to recognize December 25 as Jesus' birthday, they met resistance from some eastern Christians who complained that they already had a commemoration of Jesus' birth, and it was January 6.

And why was Epiphany on January 6? Since we know so little about other aspects of the beginning of Epiphany observances, we are uncertain about this as well. Perhaps some speculative Christian calculations convinced many followers that January 6 was the actual date of Jesus' birth or his baptism. Perhaps a widening circle of Christians followed the practice of the follow-ers of Basilides, even though the Basilidian theology was disputed. Through-out the twentieth century a widely accepted theory was that eastern Christians developed an Epiphany celebration to compete with an Egyptian winter solstice on January 6. More recent scholarship by liturgical historian Thomas Talley has raised questions about whether there really was an ancient preexisting Egyptian solstice festival on that date.[5]

Yet whether it was a solstice festival or not, it does seem that pre-Christian Egyptians had something happening on January 6. A fourth-century bishop of Cyprus, Epiphanius, who spent time as a youth in Egyptian monasteries, claimed that at Alexandria January 6 coincided with the birth of Aeon, from the virgin goddess Kore, an anniversary that the people celebrated with an all-night vigil, music, and processions carrying torches. Epiphanius also reported an Egyptian belief that on January 5 or 6 water from the Nile turned into wine. So, in Egypt, was the development of the special Christian day of Epiphany an attempt to co-opt or replace a festival already in place? Did Christian and Egyptian religious practices influence one another? I hate to keep saying this, but we do not know. Yet it seems to be a fairly good guess.

We are fairly confident in saying this: a January 6 observance of Epiphany arose and spread in the eastern church, maybe as early as the 200s, but certainly by the 300s, celebrating several ways that Jesus was made manifest in the world as the son of God. From an earlier emphasis on Jesus' baptism, the nativity story had become an increasingly central part of Epiphany by the fourth century.

ROMAN WINTER
᪥ PARTIES AND CHRISTMAS ᪢

The western church appears to have had no such Epiphany tradition. For the west, especially Rome, the first official recognition of a date as the birthday of Jesus was December 25, but such observances did not start until sometime in the fourth century. Historical surveys usually include something very brief like "the first extant reference to the Feast of the Nativity may be as old as 336."[6] Because this was such a late start for the holiday that has become so significant in the modern Christian world, I became curious to learn more about the crucial document that provides our earliest evidence. The basic facts are these.

In the West, the first written record we have that associates the birth of Jesus with December 25 is found in a Roman document called the Philocalian Calendar, also known as the Chronograph of 354, which is itself a collection of lists and records, something like an illustrated almanac. Its information was drawn from both civil and Christian sources, and it included, among other things, lists of Roman holidays, a table of dates for Easter, lists of Roman bishops and Christian martyrs, with their burial locations, a listing of the consuls of Rome, pictures of four capital cities of the Roman Empire, and pictures of emperor Constantius II and his vice emperor. Philocalus was the name of the Greek artist or engraver. The

Philocalian Calendar contained no mention of Epiphany. Also, given the Christian attitudes toward birthdays, the lists of Christian martyrs and of Roman bishops were arranged by date of death.

At two points in this document, December 25 was cited as the birth date of Christ. One mention placed it at the beginning of the list of the death dates of martyrs. Thus by that time December 25 seems to have been the beginning of the Christian liturgical calendar, and the annual listing of the death dates of martyrs would run from December 25 one year to December 25 the next year, with the birth of Christ as the key event. Yes, it seems a bit odd that the list recognized the *birth* date of Jesus but the *death* dates of the martyrs. The other mention of December 25 came in a chronological listing of the consuls of Rome. At one point in the list of consuls it says (translated into English): "Christ is born during the consulate of C. Caesar Augustus and L. Aemilianus Paulus on 25 December, a Friday, the 15th day of the new moon."[7]

The Philocalian Calendar was compiled in 354, and complicated scholarly arguments hold that selected documents within it date from 336, so it appears that by either 336 or 354, December 25 had become a recognized date for Christ's birthday in the Roman church. Because such practices seldom arise instantly in one single year, it is a reasonable presumption that Christmas observances on December 25 began somewhat earlier, but this is the first time it appears in an extant written record. Later in the fourth century, sermons and other church documents provide additional evidence that Christians were celebrating December 25 as the birth of Christ and that the practice was spreading throughout the larger church.

Although the eastern church offered some initial resistance, observance of Christ's birth on December 25 spread throughout the Christian realm in the late 300s and early 400s. It almost seems as if the eastern and western churches negotiated a trade, saying to each other, "we will adopt your observance if you adopt ours." So almost all of the eastern churches

been discussing in which the English Christmas declined dramatically, the century following the Puritan revolution. Wesley did not directly attack Christmas but said virtually nothing about it. As a matter of fact, the colonial Methodists organized the American version of their denomination at what is known as the Christmas Conference, held in Baltimore in 1784. Representatives could leave their homes, families, and friends and travel to attend this important organizational meeting because the day, December 25, was *not* a dramatically significant or holy day for them as Christians.

A Presbyterian example of opposition to Christmas is Samuel Davies, a minister in Hanover County, Virginia, who eventually became president of the College of New Jersey, later Princeton. On December 25, 1758, he complained that the Christmas season had become a time of "sinning, sexuality, luxury, and various forms of extravagance, as though men were not celebrating the birth of the holy Jesus but of Venus, or Bacchus, whose most sacred rites were mysteries of iniquity and debauchery." He said, "I do not set apart this day for public worship, as though it had any peculiar sanctity, or we were under any obligations to keep it religiously."[14] More than a century later, prominent Congregationalist preacher Henry Ward Beecher stated, "To me, Christmas is a foreign day."[15]

Even as many colonists ignored or deemphasized Christmas, many other colonists came from countries where Christmas celebrations continued. Among them were the Dutch who founded New Amsterdam (now New York), Germans colonists, and Scandinavians, as well as adherents of the Church of England who had maintained a low-key Christmas in the face of Puritan opposition. These Lutherans, Catholics, the Dutch Reformed, Anglicans (Church of England), and other small German sects brought their Christmas customs with them; their observances, whatever they were, focused upon the church or home, while normal daily activities often continued in the larger culture.

Thus, more than in England, Christmas was celebrated in the American colonies, but in a localized fashion. To understand this pattern of engaging in a religious observance while some neighbors barely noticed, think of today's American observance of Epiphany or Ash Wednesday, which are quite important to some Christians but almost unknown to other Christians. Not only do Christians' reactions to them differ, but these observances also have little impact on business patterns or the daily activities of everyone else. Rosh Hashanah or Yom Kippur, high holy days for Jews, are unnoticed by much of the Christian majority in the United States. Christmas in the colonies was something like that. It was a matter of attention only for subgroups, and it was certainly not the all-pervasive cultural and religious event that Christmas is now, in today's United States, bringing almost everything else to a standstill.

Even after the United States was formed, this situation continued well into the 1800s. Some people celebrated Christmas, but the rest of the culture did not stop. Consider these examples. Except for three years, the United States Congress met on Christmas Day every year from 1789 to 1855. Public schools met on Christmas Day in Boston, Massachusetts, at least until 1870.[16] Christmas was not a legal holiday in any state in the United States until the 1830s. The first state to make Christmas a legal holiday was Alabama, in 1836; and most other states followed in midcentury.[17]

𝕬 CHRISTMAS RETURNS 𝕭

Considering all of the cultural hoopla that now surrounds Christmas in the United States and elsewhere, obviously the snowball started rolling again at some point, gaining size and prominence once again in English speaking countries. The Christmas revival occurred in the mid-1800s, in both England and the United States. The developments in each place influenced one another, but they constitute somewhat different stories.

Of the three persons who played central roles in the resurgence of Christmas in England—Charles Dickens, Queen Victoria, and Prince

Albert—Dickens (1812–1870) is best known for his novella *A Christmas Carol*, and some people believe that through his story he virtually created Christmas.[18] That is overstated, but it is certainly true that Dickens had a key part in the English Christmas revival, and his influence on ensuing English and American conceptions of Christmas has been significant.

Dickens was interested in reports of English Christmases in earlier centuries, and he included Christmas topics in his early writings, *Sketches by Boz* and *The Pickwick Papers*. However, the major public response came when he wrote *A Christmas Carol* in 1843. The first six thousand copies of the book sold quickly, audiences were enthusiastic when he gave dramatic public readings of his story, to overflowing crowds, and ongoing sales of his book followed. He wrote four more short Christmas novels in the next five years, although none of them were as successful as *A Christmas Carol*. From 1850 to 1867 he wrote an annual Christmas short story for the two magazines he founded and edited, *Household Words* and its successor *All the Year Round*. That means that from 1843 until three years before his death, Dickens wrote a Christmas-related story almost every single year.

Yet it is *A Christmas Carol* that had the most immediate impact and the most enduring legacy. To appreciate its full importance, we must understand what Dickens accomplished with his story. Today, when we read *A Christmas Carol* or see its adaptation in plays or movies, most of us assume that, although it is a fictional story, we are also learning about what an English Christmas was like in that era. Not so. Dickens was not simply telling us about Christmas at that time; he was also trying to change it, selectively re-creating Christmas.

Think about the issue of working on Christmas Day. Today in the United States the vast majority of businesses are closed, more than at most other times of the year. Thus when Scrooge only grudgingly allowed his clerk to have Christmas Day off from work, we judge him as particularly insensitive. But in Dickens's time many businesses remained open on Christmas Day, and an indication of that reality is found in Dickens's story itself. At the end of the night, after Scrooge's heart had been changed, he threw open his window and called to a boy on the street, learned that it was Christmas Day, and asked the boy to go the poultry shop to buy a turkey. That means, of course, that both Scrooge and the boy knew the shop was open! Scrooge's earlier preference to work through Christmas Day seems more cruel to us now, with our cultural assumptions, than it would have appeared to Dickens's contemporaries. In writing his story, Dickens was an advocate in the controversies of his day, encouraging the revival or reinvention of Christmas traditions, persuading businesses to close for the holiday, and promoting acts of kindness and charity as an appropriate focus. To say it again, Dickens was *creating or revitalizing* Christmas as much as he was *reflecting* the Christmas of his time.

Most people fail to notice something else. This famous story never mentions the baby Jesus, or shepherds or wise men, or anything else about the nativity story. The only explicit mention of religion is an indication that, before Scrooge walked the streets with a new spirit on Christmas Day, he also "went to church." Three words. In light of the concern that some people express about removing Christ from Christmas, do they see Dickens as a villain because he wrote *A Christmas Carol* with virtually no mention of the birth of Jesus? What Dickens *did* advocate in his story was "the spirit of Christmas." Sociologist James Barnett has described it as Dickens's "Carol Philosophy," which "combined religious and secular attitudes toward the celebration into a humanitarian pattern. It excoriated individual selfishness and extolled the virtues of brotherhood, kindness, and generosity at Christmas. . . . Dickens preached that at Christmas men should forget self and think of others, especially the poor and the unfortunate."[19] The message was one that both religious and secular people could endorse.

As Dickens encouraged Christmas in England, he also was influential in the United States. In addition to the American sales of *A Christmas Carol*, Dickens made two American tours, one before writing the book, in 1842, when he socialized with Washington Irving (another important figure in the development of Christmas, to be discussed in the next chapter). On his second trip to the United States, in 1867, he embarked on a three-month tour presenting his famous dramatic readings of *A Christmas Carol*, drawing crowds the way rock stars do today. In Boston, 10,000 tickets were sold weeks before his appearance, and in New York 150 people stood in the cold all night long to get tickets.[20]

The influence of Dickens and his Christmas novella continued into the twentieth century and to this day, in England and America, among the famous and the general public alike. Norman Rockwell, noted especially for his *Saturday Evening Post* covers, said that listening to his father read *A Christmas Carol* aloud at the dining room table was among his fondest childhood memories. In fact, as a boy he would draw sketches as he listened, and he says that his parents decided to send him to art school after seeing a drawing of Ebenezer Scrooge that he produced on such an occasion. Franklin Delano Roosevelt read and even acted out passages of *A Christmas Carol* for his family each Christmas Eve in the White House.[21] It is because of Dickens's story that many of us today eat turkey on Christmas Day, that the name Scrooge has become a symbol of miserliness (for instance, Disney's Scrooge McDuck), and that we repeat phrases like "the spirit of Christmas," "Bah! Humbug!" and "God bless us, every one!"

In addition to Dickens, two other significant English figures in the return of Christmas were Queen Victoria and Prince Albert. The eighteen-year-old Victoria succeeded to the throne in 1837, only six years before Dickens wrote *A Christmas Carol*, and the royal couple contributed to the revival of Christmas in two major ways: importing the German Christmas tree into English Christmas observances (the snowball process at work), and modeling Christmas as a family-centered celebration.

A century earlier, in 1714, Queen Anne had died without a legitimate heir, opening the way for her German relatives, the line of Hanover, to ascend to the throne. Ensuing royalty George III, William IV, and Victoria, of partial German background themselves, also married German spouses, continuing to bring fresh German influences into Windsor Castle. As already mentioned, this is relevant to the topic of Christmas because the German people had experienced no equivalent of a Puritan suppression of Christmas, and their Christmas customs continued uninhibited. Thus, because of the German heritage of the house of Hanover, there were Christmas observances and Christmas trees in the royal family before Queen Victoria, but Victoria and Albert were the ones through whom the customs spread most visibly into the general population of England.

The influence of Victoria was more far-reaching because the public was entranced by the young queen (recall the more recent fascination with Princess Diana). After she married Albert of Saxe-Coburg-Gotha in 1840, her husband erected a Christmas tree in Windsor Castle that same year. Importing small trees directly from Coburg, Albert "turned the royal family's Christmases into semi-public events."[22] Throughout their marriage, Queen Victoria and Prince Albert also donated Christmas trees regularly for children's parties in schools and barracks. The family tree became especially famous when, on December 23, 1848, the *Illustrated London News* published an illustration of Victoria, Albert, children, and a governess, all gathered around a decorated Christmas tree that had been placed on a table, with small gifts hanging from the boughs and at the base of the tree. Here was a perfect family Christmas, a model to emulate. Christmas trees were soon the rage in England.

In 1850 a similar illustration was printed in the United States in *Godey's Lady's Book*, although Victoria's tiara and Albert's sash were edited out in this version, to make them look like an all-American family. *Godey's* was an influential publication. Its editor was Sara Josepha Hale, an arbiter of cultural taste and trends. (She also launched a crusade to make Thanksgiving a national holiday.) Illustrations of family Christmas trees continued to appear in *Godey's*, with practical suggestions about display and customs. Christmas tree illustrations began to appear in *Harper's* and elsewhere, into the Civil War period and thereafter, and the American public embraced the

Christmas symbol. By the time President Benjamin Harrison placed a tree in the White House in 1891, he called it "an old-fashioned Christmas tree."[23]

The Victorian Christmas did more than promote the Christmas tree; it centered upon the family. A Christmas revolving around children and family has become a modern American assumption, but it was not always that way. In our descriptions of earlier Christmases, notice that many Christmas festivities were adult activities, such as feasting and drinking at the village tavern, attending seasonal plays, and gathering at the parish church. Servants reversed roles with those in positions of power, and young men went from house to house, wassailing and often coercing rewards. Early, medieval, and Reformation era Christmases were more about masses at church and festivities in the village, with involvement mostly by adults, and the home was not the overwhelming focus.

Although it is difficult to trace, the Victorian era seems to be the period when the center of gravity for Christmas celebrations shifted to the home. Queen Victoria reigned in England from 1837 to 1901, an exceedingly long rule in comparison with many of her predecessors. It was the time of the British Empire's most extensive expansion across the globe, and it was a time of dramatic transformation in England itself, from agricultural life to industrial and commercial culture, and a rising middle class, with accompanying values and assumptions. So the styles, values, and tendencies of the era are what we call "Victorian," even if Queen Victoria did not directly advocate each of the trends.

This Victorian era, in addition to many other characteristics, witnessed something of a moral revival. Activists like William Wilberforce or organizations like the Society for the Suppression of Vice tried to inculcate religion and discipline among the working classes, and Queen Victoria and Prince Albert were determined to set a moral example for the aristocracy and the middle class, opposing sexual misconduct that had seemed to be the norm among previous royalty, and exhibiting concern about social problems. The era certainly had its hypocrisies and continuing gulfs between the social classes, problems that Dickens and other reformers strongly criticized, but it also was a time of moral aspirations and, some would say, even prudishness.

The family was part of this Victorian emphasis. In the words of historian Asa Briggs, "the domestic ties of the family itself were sung more loudly than at any other period of English history. . . . The home was felt to be the centre of virtues and emotions which could not be found in completed form outside." Numerous treatises were published to foster "happy families," and the family was seen as the basic, essential unit of society.[24] Victoria and Albert seemed to exemplify this theme, experiencing by almost all accounts a happy marriage and producing nine children.

A family-centered Christmas thus fit with this Victorian emphasis. Taking up the specific model provided by the royal family, with the much-reprinted illustration of Victoria, Albert, and the children gathered around the family Christmas tree, and adding the legacy of Dickens's tale, the Victorians revived or reinvented Christmas in England

It is interesting to note that the return of Christmas was *not* the result of any concerted church-based campaign. Instead, it arose from efforts by cultural leaders and drew on broader cultural forces encouraging the general themes of generosity, family activities, and festivity in the middle of winter. In the words of commentator Tom Flynn, it is "surprising how small a role the churches played in the Victorian revival. From its inception, contemporary Christmas was primarily a secular and commercial holiday. The parsons were as surprised as anyone else when after a century-long hiatus, the pews started filling up again on Christmas morning."[25]

The Christmas snowball also rolled into the American colonies and then the new United States, and, as in England, swelled incredibly in the 1800s. The English factors had an impact on the growth of the American Christmas. Yet some distinctly American factors mattered too, and most of them were involved in one way or another with one major development: the rise of Santa Claus.

four

FROM SAINT NICHOLAS TO SANTA CLAUS

✣ THE ORIGINAL SAINT ✣

Saint Nicholas probably was a real person, but we know very little else about him. Nevertheless he has become the most beloved nonbiblical saint in the history of Christianity, with endless stories and images clustered around him, stirring widespread popular devotion. As Saint Nicholas rolled through the centuries, into Europe, to America and elsewhere in the world, changing shape and characteristics along the way, he offers an ideal case study of the snowball process at work.

The *Catholic Encyclopedia* begins its entry about Nicholas succinctly, summing up our minimal historical knowledge:

> Though he is one of the most popular saints in the Greek as well as the Latin Church, there is scarcely anything historically certain about him except that he was Bishop of Myra in the fourth century. Some of the main points in his legend are as follows: He was born at Patara, a city in Lycia in Asia Minor; in his youth he made a pilgrimage to Egypt and Palestine; shortly after his return he became Bishop of Myra; cast into prison during the persecution of Diocletian, he was released after the accession of Constantine, and was present at the Council of Nicaea. In 1087 Italian merchants stole his body at Myra, bringing it to Bari in Italy.[1]

Notice that except for the general time period (the fourth century) and his location (bishop of Myra, in what is now Turkey), the encyclopedia article describes all of the rest as legend. The other information is consistent with the standard outline of Nicholas' life story, but history and legend have become so intertwined that it is virtually impossible now to tell which is which. For that reason, a papal decree in 1969 revised the Catholic liturgical calendar and demoted the feast days of ninety-two saints from "universal" to "optional," and one of the affected saints was Nicholas. No disrespect for Nicholas was intended, for he has certainly become a dearly loved figure; it was simply that so little about him can be verified historically. A few voices have even wondered if Nicholas ever existed at all, but such substantial attention was given to Nicholas within a century or two of his lifetime (bishops and popes adopting the name Nicholas, Roman emperors building significant churches in his name), it seems more plausible that all of this hoopla was based upon at least some minimal historical nuggets.

What is particularly fascinating is the collection of tales that have swirled around Nicholas. The best known is about a poor widower who feared for the future of his three daughters. Because he could not provide dowries for them, the daughters would probably not find husbands, and they would be sold into slavery or worse. Nicholas was the only child of prosperous parents, and he was determined to distribute his wealth to those in need. Nicholas learned of the family's plight, and one evening when everyone else was asleep he dropped a bag of gold through a window of their home, allowing the widower's oldest daughter to marry. Some time later Nicholas secretly dropped another bag of gold through the window for the second daughter, and still later a third bag. (Other versions say that he dropped the bags down a chimney, which may reflect more recent influences. In yet another version, one of the bags just happened to land in a stocking that a daughter had washed and hung on a mantel to dry.) When Nicholas delivered the third bag, the father was waiting, eager to learn who his benefactor was. Nicholas swore the father to secrecy, saying that thanks should go to God alone. Over the years, images of Nicholas sometimes show him holding three gold balls in his hand, representing the three bags of gold, and one tradition claims that the symbol of three balls used to designate pawnshops comes from the Nicholas legend.

Another well-known story, with many variations, tells of three boys who were sent by their father to visit Saint Nicholas for a blessing. On the way the boys stayed overnight at an inn, where the innkeeper stole their money and killed them, cutting their bodies into pieces and placing them in salt tubs, for the curing of meat. In the most grotesque version, Nicholas came to the inn and the innkeeper prepared to serve some of the very same meat to Nicholas for breakfast. Before the innkeeper could do so, Nicholas learned of the crime, confronted the innkeeper, and restored the boys to life. In one account, Nicholas raised them out of the casks not only alive but also with their clothes and money miraculously restored all at once. In other versions the boys were clerks, or theology students traveling through France, and the innkeeper was sometimes a butcher instead of an innkeeper. Based upon this story, some stained glass windows and paintings portray three small boys in a tub at the feet of Saint Nicholas.

The setting for other stories was Nicholas' trip by sea to Egypt and Palestine. When a storm arose, Nicholas calmed the seas. When a sailor fell from the ship's mast onto the deck and died, Nicholas restored him to life. Or instead, when the sailor was flung into the water and drowned, Nicholas walked on water to retrieve the sailor, carried him to the boat, and brought him back to life. One more legend told of an unscrupulous sea captain who tried to kidnap Nicholas, but a storm drove the ship toward the port at Myra, where Nicholas simply walked off the ship onto land.[2]

The miraculous tales go on and on, telling of incidents supposedly during Nicholas' life and also long after his death. For example, it is said that, even as an infant, Nicholas demonstrated his holiness by refusing to breast-feed on Wednesdays and Fridays, because these were the traditional days of fasting. Seven or eight hundred years later, Crusaders claimed to have been freed from prisons, restored to health, and blessed with visions when they prayed to Saint Nicholas. Yet from these few examples, we already can discern emerging themes: Nicholas cared for children and young people, and he was generous, a gift giver. In addition, Nicholas watched over seafarers, with several stories told about him that sound remarkably like activities previously attributed to Poseidon or Neptune. Because seafarers were both travelers and merchants, Nicholas also became the patron saint of travelers in general, and merchants, and bankers, and even pawnbrokers.

Indeed, journalist Tom Flynn has exclaimed that "Nicholas became the patron saint of damned near everything." In their book on Saint Nicholas, Joe Wheeler and Jim Rosenthal make a similar claim, noting that Nicholas becomes "all things to all people, as each age reinvents him." For the same reasons, Episcopal priest and anthropologist Earl Count called him "probably the most hard-working saint of all."[3] The key to Nicholas' popularity, I believe, has been not only his association with children and gift giving, which is important, but also his function as the equivalent of a guardian angel. For people of all ages and places, Nicholas brought comfort through the assurance that someone was watching over them and protecting them.

Thus far, we have no direct connection between Saint Nicholas and Christmas. Nicholas was simply a popular saint, particularly in the eastern church, his home region. Tradition indicated that Nicholas died on December 6, so that became the annual day on which he was remembered. As we will see, in later centuries other customs developed on Saint Nicholas' Day, such as visits to children, when Nicholas brought token presents and inquired to see if the children had been naughty or nice. However, the visits occurred on the eve and day of December 6 and were not Christmas activities. At most, you could say that the Saint Nicholas visits took place in the weeks leading up to Christmas. The seeds for a link with Christmas derived from the fact that Saint Nicholas' Day and Christmas were in the same month, and in some cultures, especially the United

States, the festivities associated with Nicholas eventually migrated across the month of December and became absorbed into Christmas.

⚘ ROLLING THROUGH EUROPE ⚘

Devotion to Saint Nicholas spread both east and west, as Christianity gained converts throughout Europe. In the east, the major push was into Slavic countries, including what is now eastern Europe, the Ukraine, Russia, and surrounding lands. The city-state Kiev served as a center of influence in the region, until Moscow took its place centuries later. The Christianity brought by missionaries included a devotion to Saint Nicholas, and by 882 a church of Saint Nicholas had been built in Kiev. Prince Oleg and his wife, Olga, became Christians, and when they signed a treaty of friendship with Constantinople in 911, among the gifts Constantinople sent in return were some relics of Saint Nicholas. Oleg and Olga's grandson was Vladimir, who ordered all the citizens of Kiev to be baptized in the Dnieper River, in one mass ceremony, and made Christianity the Russian state religion by 988. This Christian movement into Slavic lands, including Russia, had far-reaching implications up to and including the present. Approximately half of all Eastern Orthodox Christians today are Russian Orthodox.

Nicholas was a vital part of this eastern expansion. Because Russian leaders had Viking ancestors, settling in Kiev for both piracy and trade, it was understandable that they would appreciate Saint Nicholas as a patron of sailors. Thus, when virtually every Russian merchant ship carried an icon of Saint Nicholas, such devotion to him as a protector of those at sea fit well with a long-established tradition. A Serbian folksong tells an endearing little story about Nicholas at a social occasion with other saints, gathered for a drink. As summarized by Earl Count,

Saint Basil went around with a golden jug, and each saint filled his golden cup. They talked away; but Saint Nicholas began to nod, and his cup tilted in his hand. All the other saints stopped to watch him. Saint John asked, "Brother Nicholas, why are you dozing with a cup in your hand?" And Saint Nicholas roused himself and replied, "Saint John, since you ask—the enemy has raised a terrible storm in the Aegean Sea; so, while my body dozed here, my spirit was off to rescue all the ships and bring them to shore."[4]

However, most of the peoples under this Russian leadership were not sailors at all; they were peasants in the interior, with lifestyles based in agriculture and livestock. For them, Nicholas guarded the fields instead of the seas. In the words of Charles Jones, a Saint Nicholas scholar, the northerners liked Nicholas "not for his law and order, his bags of gold, his shoring up of mercantilism, but for attributes that they invented: his shepherd's friendliness, his companionship in loneliness. He became protector against wolves and wild beasts." The Russian peasants also called upon Nicholas to relieve the tyranny of the czars.[5] Here is one of our first examples of Nicholas morphing into new functions in a new geographical setting. Whether consciously or not, the Russian people invented or transmuted a popular Saint Nicholas into a figure who protected farmers and shepherds, understanding their struggles with isolation, wild animals, and tyrants.

In addition to the eastern expansion into Slavic lands, Saint Nicholas also moved west. The influence of Nicholas in western Europe received a dramatic jump start in the eleventh century, through events that seem like they should be made into a movie, both comic and tragic. A city in southeastern Italy stole the bones of Saint Nicholas from his hometown!

The year was 1087, and a group of merchants in the seaport city of Bari had been exploring ideas to enhance their municipal prestige and commerce. If they could make the city into a famous pilgrimage site where a particularly prominent saint was buried, crowds of devotees would come their way, praying in the presence of the saint's relics, seeking miracles and guidance, and, by the way, spending money. In essence, Bari wanted a religious tourist attraction. Since the city had no special saint, its citizens would have to steal one, and the tomb of Saint Nicholas at Myra seemed vulnerable, with Arab intrusions weakening the power of Constantinople in the region. Apparently Venice had the very same idea, so merchant ships from Bari raced to beat the Venetian ships to Myra. Bari won. Their landing party deceived the monks who watched over the Nicholas shrine, broke open two covers of the tomb, dug up the bones of Saint Nicholas, and carried the relics back to the ships. According to other narratives, the monks who guarded the tomb willingly gave the bones to the Bari representatives for safekeeping, fearing the depredations of Arab forces in the region, but the claim sounds to many like sugarcoating a clear case of theft. Church historians are delicate in their descriptions, seldom using terms like "robbery" or "raid" to describe how Bari acquired the body of Saint Nicholas. It has become customary to speak of the "translation" of the Nicholas relics from Myra to Bari.

The ships set sail for home, but winds pushed the boats back into the harbor. Then the captain learned that members of the raiding party had kept some bones for themselves; he searched the ships and collected all the relics into a proper casket, after which the winds shifted and the ships departed. In the view of some chroniclers of the story, Nicholas finally permitted them to leave. Contention continued when the vessels reached Bari, because the archbishop wanted the relics in his cathedral, monks wanted the bones at their monastery, and city merchants had their own ideas. The eventual decision was to build a new basilica for Saint Nicholas in Bari, and it is, to this day, one of the most majestic churches in southern Italy. Yet the final resting place for the bones of poor Saint Nicholas would be somewhat more divided. Thirteen years after Bari conducted its raid, representatives of Venice returned to Myra and dug up what they claimed to be the remaining bones of Nicholas that Bari had missed, almost 25 percent of them. On that basis, Venetians assert that *they* have Nicholas. A church in Bucharest and a monastery in Athens both claim to have Nicholas' right hand, and other locations display Nicholas' bones as well. To top it off, residents of Myra (today's Demre, Turkey) now claim that the raiders long ago were fooled into taking the wrong body, and that Demre still has the relics of Saint Nicholas.

Even so, Bari became the generally recognized location for Nicholas' remains. The plan for Bari to become a pilgrimage center worked like a charm. After the "translated" relics arrived in the city, throngs of people immediately gathered to pray for healing, and chroniclers claimed forty-seven cures in the first day alone, with twenty-two more on the second day and twenty-nine more on the third. Urban II, the very same pope whose preaching launched the First Crusade, dedicated the altar of the Basilica of Saint Nicholas in 1089. Thereafter, when many of the most famous Crusaders from throughout Europe traveled to the Holy Land, they stopped first in the port city of Bari to seek the blessing of Saint Nicholas.[6]

In addition to being a fascinating story in its own right, the relocation of Nicholas' relics to Bari accelerated the growing influence of Saint Nicholas in the West. As Crusaders and pilgrims who traveled through Bari spread the word in western Europe, the Catholic church embraced the saint as its own. In the 1100s French nuns began a practice of secretly delivering gifts to the homes of poor children on the eve of Saint Nicholas' Day, especially inspired by the story of the three daughters. The custom of gifts for children in early December proliferated in Europe, leading to the development of Saint Nicholas markets where parents could purchase toys, candy, and cookies.

Saint Nicholas observances and traditions varied from country to country, with too many examples to summarize here. The Netherlands provides an especially notable case, because much of its pattern still contin-ues today. By the 1300s Saint Nicholas already was well known in Dutch and Flemish culture. In 1516 the Netherlands fell under Spanish control, some years after the Spanish had conquered southern Italy, including Bari, and after they had pushed Arab rulers out of Spanish territory. This was an expansive era for Spain, the general period when Columbus sailed to the Americas, and Spain valued the Netherlands as an important trading center. Spain also exerted considerable influence on the Dutch Catholic church, supplying most of the church administrators and bishops. In that context, Spain became part of Dutch lore surrounding Sinter Klaas (Saint Nicholas). According to legend, Sinter Klaas spent most of the year in Spain, keeping track of the behavior of Dutch children from afar and preparing for his annual visit to the Netherlands. With Arab influence remaining among the Spanish population, Sinter Klaas had a Moorish assistant named Zwarte Piet, or Black Peter, an orphan who was pictured at times wearing a turban and a golden earring. Alternative explanations for his dark skin were that it was soot, from sliding down chimneys, or that he was a representation of the devil, who Saint Nicholas was able to conquer and force into his service. In annual observances over the years, Zwarte Piet was portrayed by a person in black face, and today some cultural commentators have criticized the legends and representations of Black Peter for racial stereotyping.

Each year, two or three weeks before Saint Nicholas' Day, Sinter Klaas and Zwarte Piet would arrive in Amsterdam by ship from Spain. Dressed as a medieval bishop, Sinter Klaas examined the children, and sometimes the adults, to see if they had behaved well, and he distributed token gifts to those who had. Black Peter provided playful comic relief and helped distribute gifts, but he also was the one assigned to deal with bad children, leaving a switch or, worse, carrying the misbehaving children away in his bag. In the evenings Sinter Klaas rode a white horse over the rooftops, leaving small gifts in wooden shoes children had placed on the step or by the fireplace. With modern adaptations, much of this pattern remains the same in the Netherlands today, still at the beginning of December, weeks prior to Christmas. This Dutch version of Saint Nicholas observances is a striking example of the snowball picking up traditions over time, starting with Saint Nicholas lore, adding remnants of the Arab presence in Spain, remnants of Spanish control of the Netherlands, a flying white horse perhaps derived from the Germanic and Nordic Odin, and Dutch clogs to receive presents, all rolled together.

Saint Nicholas met resistance in Europe in the century of the Protestant Reformation, the 1500s. One of the basic principles of the Protestant reformers was "the priesthood of all believers," declaring that each Christian had direct access to God, making mediators unnecessary. Thus, in order to pray to God or to receive God's grace, Christians did not have to rely on priests, or the Virgin Mary, or saints. In the lands that became Protestant, which was most of the northern half of Europe, many leaders were willing to continue Christmas observances, but they opposed devotion to saints as an unworthy Catholic remnant. Of course, that included Saint Nicholas. Some leaders wanted to totally eliminate any beliefs and practices about Saint Nicholas, but others, especially in Germany, proposed a substitution. Instead of having Saint Nicholas come to visit the children on the evening of December 5, why not have the Christ child do the visiting, and change the date to Christmas Eve? In that way, everything associated with Saint Nicholas' Day would be wiped away, the focus would turn to the Christ child and Christmas, and any gift giving to keep the children happy would be in a much more spiritual context. Judging by the results, it was a disastrous idea.

The first problem with a visit from the Christ child rather than Saint Nicholas was that it moved the emphasis on gifts from early December directly to the eve and day of Christmas, and many people now complain that gift giving has overwhelmed the spiritual meanings of Christmas. (We will return to that issue more than once.) The second problem was that the Christ child, sometimes portrayed by a little girl in a white dress, or never seen at all, generated little excitement from children and families, and soon the Christ child was making the rounds with Saint Nicholas or a replacement figure. In German, the child was known as the *Christkindel,* which later mutated in English to Kris Kringle, and in the United States eventually and ironically became yet another name for Santa Claus.

The third problem was that the adult figures who emerged to replace Saint Nicholas were often drawn from pre-Christian midwinter folklore that bothered some Protestants even more. In the words of one Christian commentator, turning away from Saint Nicholas "unleashed a host of semi-pagan pseudo-St. Nicholases. Instead of making the observance of Christmas more sacred, the reverse occurred."[7] A bewildering array of characters emerged, either as replacements for Saint Nicholas, or as his assistants, or as threatening counterparts who frightened children. Stand-ins for Nicholas himself included *Weihnachtsmann* (Christmas man) in Germany, Old Man Winter in Finland, and Father Christmas in England. Sinter Klaas held on tenaciously in the Netherlands, deflecting all substitutes. Other, sometimes frightening, winter visitors carried over from pre-Christian times included the witchlike Belfana in Italy, and both Knecht Ruprecht and Berchta in German lands.

☃ HERE COMES SANTA CLAUS ☃

Within a century of the Protestant Reformation and its turmoil, Europeans began to establish colonies on the eastern shores of North America. A glimmer of a Saint Nicholas memory slipped across the waters along with the colonists, and the new setting would produce a mutation that overwhelmed all that came before.

It was in the United States, particularly New York, that Saint Nicholas became Santa Claus. Although the development of any tradition is the result of many influences, one way to describe the emergence of Santa Claus is to chart the cumulative additions and transformations by six notable contributors: John Pintard, Washington Irving, Clement Clarke Moore (or perhaps Henry Livingston Jr.), Thomas Nast, Francis Church, and Haddon Sundblom. To return to the snowball image we have been using, these six persons each had a turn at pushing the snowball along, adding new features in the process.

For background, remember the mixed attitudes toward Christmas in the American colonies, discussed in the last chapter. While the Puritans and several other English speaking-denominations discouraged Christmas, other colonial Christians, such as the Dutch and the Germans, continued to celebrate it more fully. Thus, we might expect that early developments in an American transformation of Saint Nicholas would come from a region colonized by the Dutch or the Germans, and indeed that is what happened. The first five persons in the list were from New York, begun as New Amsterdam, and even more, the first three were members of the very same organization, the New York Historical Society.

John Pintard. The first person to push the snowball was John Pintard (1759–1844), a merchant and philanthropist who lived most of his life in New York City and was involved in numerous civic projects. He was the founder of New York's first savings bank, founder of the American Bible Society, secretary of the American Academy of Fine Arts, and secretary of the New York Chamber of Commerce. He agitated for a free public school system, was involved in the movement to build the Erie Canal, and worked to establish Washington's Birthday, the Fourth of July, and Columbus Day as national holidays. In addition to all of these other activities, in November 1804 Pintard gathered eleven prominent New York leaders, including Mayor DeWitt Clinton, for a preliminary meeting to organize the New York Historical Society, and when the group elected officers in 1805, Pintard was its first secretary.

Members of the New York Historical Society were not necessarily Dutch, but the early heritage of their city obviously was, and from the society's beginning Pintard saw Saint Nicholas as a symbol of those Dutch roots. At the society's annual banquet in January 1809, Dr. David Hosack gave this toast: "To the memory of St. Nicholas. May the virtuous habits and simple manners of our Dutch ancestors be not lost in the luxuries and refinements of the present time."[8] Under Pintard's leadership, the New York Historical Society began an annual Saint Nicholas Day dinner on December 6, 1810, and for the occasion Pintard commissioned a woodcut illustration of Nicholas, clothed in a bishop's robes. The Saint Nicholas snowball began to roll!

Washington Irving. Interestingly, at the same 1809 banquet Pintard's brother-in-law, none other than Washington Irving, was nominated for membership in the New York Historical Society, and his influence regarding Nicholas would become more significant than Pintard's. In the words of historian Stephen Nissenbaum, "If it was John Pintard who introduced the figure of St. Nicholas, it was Washington Irving who popularized it." Called "the first internationally known American author," at least of fiction, Washington Irving (1783–1859) is best known among most Americans for his stories "Rip Van Winkle" and "The Legend of Sleepy Hollow."[9] Irving's publications were voluminous, and one that contributed to the Nicholas tradition was a satirical history of New York, intended as a parody of *The Picture of New York* by Samuel Latham Mitchell, a volume that Irving found pretentious. Irving wrote the epic under the pseudonym Diedrich Knickerbocker when he was only twenty-four, and the title itself, in its long version, should alert readers to its whimsical nature:

A History of New York
From the Beginning of the World to the End of the Dutch Dynasty
Containing, Among Many Surprising and Curious Matters,

The Unutterable Ponderings of Walter the Doubter,
The Disastrous Projects of William the Testy, and
The Chivalric Achievements of Peter the Headstrong
The Three Dutch Governors of New Amsterdam
Being the Only Authentic History of the Times that Ever Hath Been
    or Ever Will Be Published
By Diedrich Knickerbocker

The name "Knickerbocker" refers to knickers, short pants gathered at the knee, worn by the Dutch. Because of the fame of Irving's pseudonym, Knickerbocker became a nickname for residents of the city and the state of New York, which in turn led much later to the name for the professional basketball team the New York Knicks.

Irving published Knickerbocker's *History* on Saint Nicholas' Day 1809, and it contained twenty-five references to Saint Nicholas, describing the importance of Nicholas in the lives of the residents of New Amsterdam. Irving claimed that the ship *Goede Vrouw*, carrying Dutch immigrants, included a figurehead of Nicholas on its bow: "a goodly image of St. Nicholas, equipped with a low, broad-brimmed hat, a huge pair of Flemish trunk-hose, and a pipe that reached to the end of the bowsprit." Irving wrote that the first church in the Dutch colony was named for Saint Nicholas, and he described the festivities surrounding Saint Nicholas' Day as a special focus in the life of New Amsterdam. As portrayed by Irving, Saint Nicholas flew over trees in a horse-pulled wagon and slid down chimneys to deliver gifts. When one character, Oloffe Van Kortlandt, had a dream about Saint Nicholas, at least one of Irving's phrases sounds very familiar to modern readers, because it would later be included almost verbatim in a more famous poem: "And when St. Nicholas had smoked his pipe, he twisted it in his hat-band, and laying his finger beside his nose, gave the astonished Van Kortlandt a very significant wink, then, mounting his wagon, he returned over the tree-tops and disappeared."[10]

In more recent years, these descriptions have ignited a debate among historians, because some have accepted Irving's account at face value, including in their own histories Irving's information about how important Saint Nicholas was to the Dutch colony. Others are skeptical, reminding us that the Knickerbocker *History* was intended to be a satire. After examining external historical evidence, Charles W. Jones, a Saint Nicholas specialist, concluded that the Nicholas items in Irving's book were "all sheer fictions." "When we look at the available documents—that is, the newspapers, magazines, diaries, books, broadsides, music, visual aids, and merchandise of the past," Jones wrote, there was no observance of Saint Nicholas' Day in the Dutch colony, no Nicholas figurehead on the ship, "no dedication of the first church to *any* saint, no iconography, no pipe," no reference to Saint Nicholas as their patron saint.[11] Jones argued that Saint Nicholas traditions were a matter of contention in the Netherlands in the era of the Protestant Reformation, and the colonists did not bring Nicholas with them when they came to the Americas. Thus, we should see the Nicholas references as Irving's whimsical creation rather than as a reflection of early colonial realities.

In essence, Saint Nicholas in the colony of New Amsterdam was an invented tradition, attributable to Irving and his acquaintances. Members of the New York Historical Society liked the tradition, and by 1835 Washington Irving and others founded the Saint Nicholas Society of New York City. On the role of Irving in this developing tradition, Charles Jones wrote, "Without Washington Irving there would be no Santa Claus."[12]

Another of Irving's works, *The Sketch Book of Geoffrey Crayon, Gent.* (1819–20), which contained the famous stories about Rip Van Winkle and Ichabod Crane, also included five sketches of how Christmas was observed at a manor in England called Bracebridge Hall, remembering Christmases of earlier times. Supposedly based upon information gleaned during Irving's travels in England, these descriptions fascinated both English and American readers and played a role in the overall revival of Christmas in both countries in the early nineteenth century. Yet the Bracebridge descriptions have touched off the same kind of disagreements among historians that have raged about Knickerbocker's *History* and Dickens's Christmas writings. How much did they describe historical practices, and how much did they establish new customs, bathing them in the veneer of nostalgia by portraying them as traditions from the past? As in most debates, there is some truth on each side, but clearly both Dickens and Irving were involved in constructing and molding Christmas traditions.

Clement Moore or Henry Livingston. The third step in the development of an American Santa Claus came with the famous and incredibly influential poem popularly called "The Night Before Christmas," first published, anonymously, in the Troy, New York, *Sentinel* in 1823. The generally accepted author is Clement Clarke Moore (1779–1863), who was yet another member of the New York Historical Society, a personal acquaintance of both Pintard and Irving, and part of New York's elite. His mother's family, the Clarkes, owned a large country estate called Chelsea that Clement Moore inherited, covering the area still identified as the Chelsea district in Manhattan, north of Greenwich Village. (It is difficult now to imagine Manhattan without unending skyscrapers, but in Moore's time most settlement was in the southern part of the island, and the Chelsea estate was basically out in the country.) Clement Moore's father was the Episcopal priest who offered communion to the dying Alexander Hamilton after his famous duel with Aaron Burr. His father also served as the Episcopal bishop of the New York diocese for thirty-five years and as president of Columbia College, later Columbia University. Clement Moore was wealthy enough that he never needed a job, although he taught part-time as a professor of Oriental and Greek literature at General Theological Seminary, an Episcopal school he helped found on a portion of Chelsea's land.

The Moore family testified that Clement Clarke Moore wrote the now-famous poem for his children, and that he would recite it from memory for his family during the Christmas season. Accounts vary in explaining how the *Sentinel* obtained a copy of the poem, usually assuming that a friend or family member copied the poem from the family album and then provided it anonymously to the newspaper's editor. It was reprinted elsewhere, and by the 1830s it really took off. Moore finally claimed its authorship, in print, in a multiauthor collection of poems in 1837 and in an anthology of his own poetry in 1844.

However, the family of Revolutionary War veteran Henry Livingston, Jr. (1748–1828) claimed that he wrote the poem. Its 1823 anonymous publication came in the latter years of Livingston's life, and he never publicly claimed its authorship. As the poem gained popularity, his family argued that he had written it in the first decade of the 1800s for his children, and that a governess for the Moores had heard Livingston recite the poem and asked for a copy. Livingston wrote other poetry that sounds remarkably similar to the Christmas poem, and the family claimed that Livingston's temperament and style fit "The Night Before Christmas" much better than Moore's work did. Descendants and scholars on both sides still argue about the issue of authorship, and the disagreement was heightened in 2000 when a book by Don Foster, a Vassar College English professor who specializes in linguistic analysis, took the side of the Livingstons. The arguments back and forth are fascinating, but it seems like the kind of dispute that may never be settled, akin to debates about whether all of Shakespeare's plays were really written by Shakespeare, or who really assassinated President Kennedy. To sample arguments on both sides, investigate the sources in the backnote for this paragraph.[13]

Whoever wrote the poem, it has assumed an immensely important role in the development of the American Santa Claus. We could give it credit for a number of "firsts," for example, the first to place Santa in a sleigh, with reindeer, and the first to give the reindeer names. Yet historians have discovered another possible source, a little-known poem published in 1821, that may preempt some of the claims. If Livingston wrote the "The Night Before Christmas" before 1810, it still would be first. If Moore wrote it in 1822, with its anonymous publication in 1823, then it is likely that Moore borrowed ideas from the earlier 1821 poem. The 1821 poem was part of a projected series of children's books called *The Children's Friend*, published in New York by William Gilley, an acquaintance of Moore's, but the engraving and poem are anonymous. The somewhat crude drawing put Saint Nicholas, or Santa Claus, on a rooftop, in a sleigh pulled by one reindeer. The poem referred to "Old Santeclaus" and said that he brought yearly gifts on Christmas Eve. Even if this poem came first, it was not widely reprinted. By itself, its innovations, including the notion of a sleigh and a reindeer, might have drifted into oblivion. It was "The Night Before Christmas" that was embraced by the public, resonating with a popular audience and launching a phenomenon.

"The Night Before Christmas" is the best-known poem in the English language. If someone gave us its first line, most of us could recite the second line automatically. Yet most of us are not aware of how dramatically important this poem was in reshaping both Saint Nicholas and the American Christmas. When I listened to "The Night Before Christmas" as a child, and even reading it later as an adult, I assumed that the picture of Santa Claus I had in my mind, a jolly plump man appearing on Christmas Eve, in a red and white outfit, with a twinkle in his eye, riding in a flying sleigh pulled by reindeer, was already a well-developed tradition, and the author simply wrote an appealing, catchy poem about it. Not so. This poem helped *create* vital parts of the Santa Claus tradition, and other parts of the tradition would be added later. Even if we assume that Moore wrote the poem, which would place its composition after Irving's Knickerbocker *History of New York* and after *The Children's Friend* publication, this is what the poem created:

First of all, Saint Nicholas traveled in a sleigh, not riding a horse or in a wagon. The 1821 *Children's Friend* poem may have introduced a sleigh, but "The Night Before Christmas" popularized it.

Second, the sleigh was pulled by a team of reindeer, and they were given names. The 1821 poem had one reindeer, but "The Night Before

Christmas" had eight, and it named them Dasher, Dancer, Prancer, Vixen, Comet, Cupid, Donder (later changed to Donner), and Blitzen. We really have no idea where the idea of reindeer came from; no portrayal of Saint Nicholas in Europe associated him with reindeer. One idea is that in the seventeenth century, when the Russian Orthodox brought Saint Nicholas to Siberia, a region that included native people who depended upon reindeer, perhaps an association developed there. However, no historian or ethnographer has yet been able to make the case. A better speculation might come from Norse mythology, where the thunder god Thor rode a flying chariot pulled by the magical goats Gnasher and Cracker.[14] All of these suggestions are guesses. The source of the reindeer for Saint Nicholas mythology remains a mystery.

Third, Saint Nicholas came on Christmas Eve. The observances encouraged by John Pintard and the writings of Washington Irving celebrated the coming of Saint Nicholas on December 5, the eve of Saint Nicholas' Day, as celebrated in Holland. In this poem, and in *The Children's Friend*, Nicholas migrated to Christmas and became a key part of Christmas festivities. This was huge! Think of the far-reaching implications, especially for the association of gift giving with Christmas.

Fourth, Saint Nicholas lost his bishop's robe and mitered cap; you might say he was defrocked. In Europe the Dutch Saint Nicholas appeared as a bishop, and he retained a similar appearance in the drawing commissioned by Pintard in 1810. Washington Irving provided some changes, giving Saint Nicholas a broad-brimmed hat, a pipe, and Flemish "trunk-hose." Yet "The Night Before Christmas" was even more intent on creating an endearing figure. "St. Nick" became a cute, loveable little man, like a favorite uncle or grandfather, but magical.

His eyes—how they twinkled! His dimples how merry!
His cheeks were like roses, his nose like a cherry!

His droll little mouth was drawn up like a bow,

. . . .

He had a broad face and a little round belly,
That shook when he laughed, like a bowl full of jelly.
He was chubby and plump, a right jolly old elf,
And I laughed when I saw him, in spite of myself.

Fifth, relieved of his role as an authority figure, he no longer threat-ened punishment. Many of Saint Nicholas' visits in Europe brought rewards for children who were good and a switch or a lump of coal for those who were not. The 1821 poem still included threats for children who were bad; historian Stephen Nissenbaum calls it "a mini-version of the Day of Judgment."[15] The well-known Christmas song "Santa Claus Is Coming to Town" warns that "he knows if you've been bad or good, so be good for goodness sake," a remnant of the theme of discipline. Unlike it, "The Night Before Christmas" contains not even a hint of punishment, making clear that there is "nothing to dread."

Hence this poem did far more than add some reindeer and name them. It transported Saint Nicholas across the month of December to Christ-mas, and it transformed him from the authority figure of a bishop into a nonjudgmental jolly gift giver. Is it any wonder that children and families embraced him?

Additional features of Saint Nicholas were yet to come. First of all, notice that this poem included no references to Santa Claus. He was still Saint Nicholas, and in one case "St. Nick." However, in the broader New York culture the related names were already becoming interchangeable, simply as a process of bringing a Dutch Sinter Klaas into the English language. A poem published in 1810 referred to "Sancte Claus," and the 1821 *Children's Friend* poem described "Old Santeclaus." When the Troy *Sentinel* republished "The Night Before Christmas" in 1830, again anonymously, the editor gave it the title "An Account of a Visit from St. Nicholas, or Santa Claus," even though the words Santa Claus never appear in the poem. Clement Moore preferred the title "A Visit from St. Nicholas."

As an additional curiosity, most people do not notice that in the poem, Saint Nicholas is little, an elf, not a full-sized person. Significant phrases refer to a "*miniature* sleigh," "eight *tiny* reindeer," "a *little* old driver," "each *little* hoof," "his droll *little* mouth," "a *little* round belly," and "a right jolly old *elf.*" (That would explain, by the way, how he could go up and down chimneys.) When the poem was first published as an illustrated book, the accompanying illustration featured someone who looked like a scruffy leprechaun. Today, many illustrated children's book versions of this poem contain images of an adult-sized Santa that do not fit with the words, anachronistically importing later visual representations. When this poem was written, Santa Claus had not yet reached his modern appearance.

Thomas Nast. Three more key persons helped put the finishing touches on the modern Santa Claus. One was yet another New Yorker, Thomas Nast (1840–1902), who was born in Germany but immigrated with his family to America when he was six years old. Nast became a prominent cartoonist and illustrator, working as the head cartoonist at *Harper's Weekly* for thirty years. He invented both the Republican elephant and the Democratic donkey as political party emblems, and he had a role in developing the symbol of Uncle Sam. Even with those notable contributions, the drawings that established his greatest legacy were of Santa Claus.

As drawn by Nast, Santa's jolly face, full beard, and wide belt around his rotund waist established an image that endures to this day, bringing life to the character described in "The Night Before Christmas." Santa's height would vary in Nast's illustrations, but he still tended to be short. The outfit that Nast gave Santa was a little different from our modern image, with a fur hat rather than a stocking cap, and clothes ("dressed all in fur, from his head to his foot") that looked like *very* itchy long underwear. Nast returned to the subject of Santa year after year in *Harper's*, and the content of his drawings added many other lasting features to the Santa mythology:

- a North Pole headquarters
- Santa as a toymaker, in his North Pole workshop
- elves as Santa's assistants
- Santa receiving letters from children
- Santa's giant ledgers to record children's names
- snacks left in homes on Christmas Eve for Santa

A picture is worth a thousand words, they say; through his illustrations, Nast substantially expanded the lore about Santa.

Francis Church. Another major contributor to the growing Santa Claus phenomenon, measured by popular response, was a newspaper editorial written in answer to a child's question. In the fall of 1897 the *New York Sun* received a letter from an eight-year-old girl, Virginia O'Hanlon, asking if there really was a Santa Claus. Her mailing address was West 95th Street, New York City (where else?). An editorial writer quickly wrote a response in one afternoon, and its initial appearance on September 21, 1897, was nothing special. "It was the seventh article on the page and ran below commentaries on New York and Connecticut politics, the strength of the British navy, chainless bicycles, and a Canadian railroad to the Yukon."[16] It was not even published during the Christmas season. The editorial was picked up and reprinted seemingly everywhere, and the *New York Sun* began a tradition of republishing the editorial every year until the newspaper went out of business in 1950. Movies, a musical, and even a cantata were based on the instant journalistic classic, "Yes, Virginia, There Is a Santa Claus."

The *New York Sun* did not identify the author of its editorials with a byline, so only upon the death of Francis Pharcellus Church (1839–1906) did the public learn his name. He was a lifelong journalist, the son of a

Baptist minister, and had no children. Church's editorial appealed to faith and mystery, arguing that many aspects of life merit belief even when we cannot see them.

> Virginia, your little friends are wrong. They have been affected by the skepticism of a skeptical age. They do not believe except they see. . . .
>
> Yes, Virginia, there is a Santa Claus. He exists as certainly as love, and generosity, and devotion exist, and you know that they abound and give to your life its highest beauty and joy. Alas! How dreary would be the world if there were no Santa Claus! It would be as dreary as if there were no Virginia. There would be no childlike faith, then, no poetry, no romance to make tolerable this existence. We should have no enjoyment, except in sense and sight. The Eternal light with which childhood fills the world would be extinguished. . . .
>
> Only faith, fancy, poetry, love, romance, can push aside [the veil covering the unseen] . . . and picture the supernal beauty and glory beyond. Is it all real? Ah, Virginia, in all this world there is nothing else real and abiding.[17]

Critics have attacked the editorial for advocating blind faith, and it did indeed argue for "childlike faith" although, it should be noted, nothing explicitly Christian. Church's opinion piece contained no reference to the birth of Jesus or any part of the nativity story. It was a child-centered editorial, but the little essay clearly resonated with a general public of all ages, arguably because adults also yearned for a sense of wonder.

By the late 1800s, images of and references to Santa Claus appeared in children's books, games, songs, dolls, newly introduced Christmas cards, and magazine and newspaper advertisements. Tall or short, thin or plump, Santa was dressed in fur or cloth, with colors varying from red and blue to earth tones. Red became the most common color for his clothing, and department store Santas appeared with standard red and white costumes, although the uniformity was not absolute. An editorial in the November 27, 1927, *New York Times* described both the variations and the emerging common pattern:

In other years children who went from one store to another frequently were disturbed by a succession of Santa Clauses of different sizes and figures—tall and thin, short and fat, lean, burly and nondescript. Parents this year will be less hard put to it to explain why one Santa Claus differs from another, for one type is in demand. Height, weight, stature are almost as exactly standardized as are the red garments, the hood, the white whiskers, and the pack full of toys. Ruddy cheeks and nose, bushy white eyebrows and a jolly paunchy effect are also inevitable parts of the requisite make-up.[18]

One additional artist would help complete the standardization.

Haddon Sundblom. Active half a century after Thomas Nast, Haddon Sundblom (1899–1976) established himself as a Chicago-based commercial artist. In addition to illustrating fiction for the *Saturday Evening Post* and *Ladies' Home Journal,* he painted images for a long list of advertising clients: "Cream of Wheat and Nabisco Shredded Wheat cereals, Aunt Jemima pancake mix, Maxwell House coffee, Palmolive, Cashmere Bouquet and Camay soaps, Whitman chocolates, Goodyear tires, Four Roses whiskey, Budweiser, Schlitz, Lone Star and Pabst beers, the U.S. Marine Corps, and many car makers, including Ford, Packard, Lincoln, Buick, Pierce-Arrow, and Jordan."[19]

His best-known art was created for an additional client, Coca-Cola. The Coca-Cola Company hired a number of prominent illustrators for its advertising, including Norman Rockwell and N. C. Wyeth, but Sundblom became the artist the company relied upon most, painting scenes portraying Coca-Cola in many settings, from beaches to soda fountains. From 1931 to 1964 he produced at least one Coca-Cola Santa Claus painting every year, and between 1944 and 1953 there were two or three Santa paintings annually. This advertising initiative made sense: if an association of Coca-Cola with Santa Claus could boost winter seasonal sales, the company would be that much more successful. Also, building an association with a red and white Santa was ideal for a soft drink whose emblematic colors were, come to think of it, red and white! "By 1940, The Coca-Cola Company was, in its own words, 'the outstanding poster [i.e., billboard] advertiser in the country,' ensuring massive exposure for the yearly Santa, who also appeared in a blizzard of magazine ads and other media."[20]

A common urban legend claims that Coca-Cola invented Santa Claus. Clearly, on the basis of all the preceding influences described here, that is not true. Haddon Sundblom may have polished Santa a little, confirming him as an adult-sized figure, with plush clothing and fur trimming instead of a cheap costume. Other illustrators like Norman Rockwell and Joseph Leyendecker played a role as well. Although Sundblom helped put the finishing touches on a Santa Claus who already had become mostly standardized, his more significant contribution came through the cumulative impact of more than thirty years of billboards, magazine advertisements, and full-sized cardboard figures in stores, still continuing their influence as Coca-Cola Santa collectibles of trays, posters, and figurines. Utter the words "Santa Claus," and a single image arises in virtually every American's mind. The person who froze that image in place, through Coca-Cola advertising, was Haddon Sundblom. In the words of Gerry Bowler, who wrote a "biography" of Santa Claus, Sundblom "made a familiar image even more likeable and widespread." "The overwhelming ubiquity of these advertisements . . . ensured that no rival version of Santa could emerge in the North American consciousness."[21]

⚜ THE MEANINGS OF SANTA ⚜

The long journey from Saint Nicholas to Santa Claus prompts several observations. First, it illustrates the way in which folk and popular traditions morph and borrow from one another as they move through cultures and through time. It can be hard to describe exactly the stages of development, especially in earlier eras, but we can see broad changes and modifications.

One discernable pattern is Saint Nicholas' progression through three major roles: protector, disciplinarian, and gift giver. All three roles were present in the beginning, but the shifts in emphasis have been dramatic. In the first thousand years, when Nicholas became the patron saint of practically everyone, he functioned especially as a *protector,* based upon belief in his miraculous powers. He saved children, seafarers, peasants, and Crusaders. Then in the later Middle Ages and the Reformation, he became especially associated with regular home visits on or before Saint Nicholas' Day and focused increasingly on children and their behavior, rewarding the good and threatening the bad. While he still might offer protection and also bring token gifts, the emphasis was upon Nicholas as *disciplinarian.* Even when reformers tried to diminish his role, his various cultural replacements continued to perform very similar functions. With the exception of some secularized replacements in Protestant countries, Nicholas carried out both of the first two roles as a religious figure. The third emphasis rose with the American development of Santa Claus. He lost his religious authority and became a kindly, even jolly, grandfather figure who delivered presents, a *gift giver.* It is the third function that now dominates the American Christmas holiday.

Especially when we move beyond folk traditions and get to the point where we can identify specific people who shaped public notions of Saint Nicholas–Santa Claus, we can ask two basic questions. Why did the originators create what they did, and why did the general public make it popular? As an example of the first basic question: in the case of Pintard, Irving, and Moore, who were in the same social circle, why did they want to promote a celebration of Saint Nicholas? What motivated them? Historian Stephen Nissenbaum has argued that these three, as members of New York's elite, "felt that they belonged to a patrician class whose authority was under siege," and the feeling was accented at Christmastime when roving bands of rowdy youth engaged in genuinely threatening behavior under the guise of wassailing.[22] Thus, initiating Saint Nicholas traditions could be a means of social control, redirecting Christmas festivities to domestic, child-centered activities in the home as a way to combat or marginalize the carousing in the streets.

It is a stimulating, provocative thesis, one I find partially persuasive, but I also think the second basic question is even more important. Why did the public embrace Saint Nicholas, or the revised version as Santa Claus? For example, other members of the elite might publish poems or stories they hoped would change society, but if the poems were ignored, the writers' motives would not matter. Although it is interesting to wonder what Moore or Livingston had in mind in composing "The Night Before Christmas," I think it is equally important, if not more so, to ask why the public loved the poem, and why it has become such an enduring classic. Is it simply our greed, because we like gifts? Is it the appeal of a kindly figure who does not threaten us? Is it an embrace of children and domestic ideals? Is it a sense of awe and wonder? Is it about generosity?

We should keep these kinds of questions in mind as we approach the next chapter, about the commercialization of Christmas. It is tempting to launch into tirades against Santa Claus as a symbolic villain, seducing shoppers into consumerist excesses, drowning people in bankruptcies and subverting human values. Indeed, Santa *has* been manipulated by commercial interests for the sake of sales and profit. But if that is all Santa is, what do we do with the tremendous response to Francis Church's *New York Sun* editorial? Those who love to reread the words to Virginia, or those who watch *Miracle on 34th Street* every Christmas, obviously embrace Santa Claus for reasons other than consumerism, perhaps including generosity, wonder, miracles, joy, and a generalized "spirit of Christmas." Regarding all topics in the history of Christmas, it is instructive to ask, why was this tradition or practice created, and perhaps more important, why did the public respond the way it did?

One final observation on the rise of Santa Claus also helps explain the expansion of the cultural importance of Christmas in nineteenth-century America. If Christmas revived in England in the 1800s, it *really* took off in the United States. In addition to Dickens's "spirit of Christmas" and Victorian influences, it was the American Santa Claus who made the difference, emerging as the central icon of the season, around whom everyone could rally. Both the religious and nonreligious public could embrace a Santa who brought joy to children and families, who represented a spirit of giving and the nonjudgmental warmth of good feeling among all people. Even business interests could add their encouragement, because Santa as gift giver held so many commercial possibilities. And it all still served as a winter party, bringing lights and celebration in the midst of the cold and dark. With Santa's encouragement, now the entire culture stopped for the Christmas parade.

The ancient Roman Saturnalia. Undated illustration. © Bettmann/CORBIS

Charles Dickens giving a reading, 1870 engraving. © Bettmann/CORBIS

Mr. Fezziwig's Ball. John Leech's illustration from Charles Dickens,
A Christmas Carol, 1843. © Historical Picture Archive/CORBIS

Queen Victoria and Prince Albert at Christmas.
Illustrated London News, December 1848. © Bettmann/CORBIS

Children bringing home a Christmas tree. Engraving circa 1870.
© Bettmann/CORBIS

Saint Nicholas of Myra. Drawing after a triptych by Matthew Grunewald.
© Bettmann/CORBIS

Kriss Kringle's Christmas Tree. Woodcut title page, 1845. © CORBIS

SANTA CLAUS OR ST. NICHOLAS, THE PATRON OF NEW YORK.

Santa Claus, patron of New York. Undated engraving. © Bettmann/CORBIS

"Merry old Santa Claus," by Thomas Nast. 1881 engraving.
© Bettmann/CORBIS

Scene from *It's a Wonderful Life*. James Stewart and Lionel Barrymore.
© Bettmann/CORBIS

Movie cast of *White Christmas*. Bing Crosby, Rosemary Clooney, Vera-Ellen, Danny Kaye. © Underwood & Underwood/CORBIS

five

AND THEN
THERE WAS
MONEY

In 1892 William Dean Howells wrote a now-classic short story entitled "Christmas Every Day," in which a child learned that it might be unwise to wish that every day was Christmas. A scene early in the story evokes a common vision of Christmas morning:

> She waited around till the rest of the family were up, and she was the first to burst into the library, when the doors were opened, and look at the large presents laid out on the library-table—books, and portfolios, and boxes of stationery, and breast-pins, and dolls, and little stoves, and dozens of handkerchiefs, and ink-stands, and skates, and snow-shovels, and photograph-frames, and little easels, and boxes of water-colors, and Turkish paste, and nougat, and candied cherries, and dolls' houses, and waterproofs,—and the big Christmas-tree, lighted and standing in a waste-basket in the middle.[1]

That was not the end of it; stockings held more gifts, and additional presents "poured in" throughout the morning. Some details in this scene represent Christmas in Howells's era rather than American customs today, because the gifts and the tree were on a table, not on the floor, and the presents were not wrapped. Yet the overall picture, drowning in gifts, feels very familiar to many Americans even now and symbolizes what has been called the commercialized American Christmas.

Whatever the winter festival and religious roots of Christmas, and whatever its variations over nearly two thousand years, almost everyone acknowledges that Christmas in the United States today has become overwhelmed by the commercial elements of the holiday. Expenditures are massive, for gifts, food, decorations, and activities. "Black Friday," the Friday after Thanksgiving, is so called because it is the traditional beginning of the Christmas shopping season and is supposedly the time when many businesses move from the red into the black, the entire profit margin for the year depending upon Christmas-related sales. Whether or not that claim is entirely accurate, it indicates the major importance of the Christmas season in the American economy, and the great impact commerce has upon the way Christmas is celebrated.

This reality begs the question of when and why gifts and other purchases became such an important part of the holiday. How are we to evaluate the intertwined relationship of Christmas and consumerism?

⚵ THE RISE OF CONSUMERISM ⚵

To summarize the historical development of the modern commercialized Christmas, let me begin with seven generalizations. Once we glimpse the story's broad sweep, we can always puzzle out complexities and exceptions.

1. *Before the nineteenth century, gifts were not the focus of Christmas observances.* Even in the pre-Christian Roman Saturnalia and the January Kalends, people spent most of their time and money on food, alcohol, games, and general frivolity, and any gifts tended to be tokens. When Christmas began, and on through the medieval and Reformation periods, the festivities consisted mainly of village gatherings, feasts, and special masses for the birth of Christ. Royalty might sponsor some lavish celebrations with elaborate gifts, but for the average person Christmas centered on food, parties, worship, perhaps a holiday from work, and as a minimal part, small gifts for children or family. Any other gifts tended to be obligations between groups of different social status, such as rulers to their subjects, or vice

versa, rather than signs of affection. For example, in medieval England peasants would bring harvested produce as gifts to the lord of their estate, and the lord in return would sponsor a feast. For most of Christian history, if items were bartered or money spent at Christmastime, it usually was about food and alcohol, not the extensive gift giving so familiar today.

2. *Industrialization in the 1700s and 1800s helped lead to the rise of consumer culture.* With factories and other forms of specialized production, instead of an economy based upon artisans and farmers, industrialization created all kinds of commodities. More production made it important for merchants to stimulate more demand, through advertising and marketing. The result was a culture that encouraged people to dress in the latest fashions, to dream about luxurious possessions, and to buy goods and services once produced at home. A commodity-centered culture would have an impact on Christmas.

3. *Soon enough, merchants began to see holidays as an opportunity rather than an obstacle. That included Christmas.* The older business approach to holidays—akin to the seventeenth-century Puritans' view that they gave occasions for idleness—was voiced in Dickens's *Christmas Carol* by Scrooge, who complained that Christmas was "a poor excuse for picking a man's pocket," because he had to "pay a day's wages for no work." When Christmas revived in the 1800s in England and in the United States, a change in business attitudes helped the resurgence. In an interesting phrase from historian Leigh Schmidt, the Victorian revival of Christmas allowed retailers to make a "modern recalculation of the economic benefits of holiday observance."[2]

4. *Earlier gift-giving traditions, associated with Saint Nicholas' Day and New Year's Day, shifted across the American calendar to Christmas in the mid 1800s.* In the historical journey from Saint Nicholas to Santa Claus, many cultures included at least token gift giving on December 5, the eve of Saint Nicholas' Day, and some New Yorkers were interested in continuing the observance in the United States. In addition, gifts as part of New Year's festivities had a

long heritage in Europe and that tradition was carried into the United States. Some people referred to New Year's gifts as "Christmas presents" because New Year's Day fell within the twelve days of Christmas, but in spite of the name they still were gifts given on January 1.

Yet in the middle of the nineteenth century, for reasons that are unclear, gift traditions associated with the other two days declined in the United States. Chapter 4 explained that the popular embrace of the poem "The Night Before Christmas" helped shift Saint Nicholas–Santa Claus gifts to Christmas, but why did New Year's gifts coalesce there too? Perhaps it was an attempt to shorten a prolonged holiday period of a week or more, concentrating instead on Christmas. Maybe people believed that the religious associations of Christmas, or its associations with family, could help keep the potential excesses of gift giving in check. If that was the motivation, it does not seem to have succeeded.

5. *Manufactured, purchased Christmas gifts began to replace homemade ones in the United States in the late 1800s and early 1900s.* This is partly the story of an America in transition from rural, agrarian roots to an increasingly urban and industrialized culture. In rural areas, winter allowed time for men to carve wooden toys and women to bake and sew, and the handmade gifts were special because each one was unique and represented a personal investment of time by the giver. The gifts highlighted personal relationships, and their price was not an issue.

Manufactured gifts eventually became more widespread for several reasons. As industrial laborers had less time to make presents, purchases were more convenient and easily available in urban settings. Retailers in smaller towns and mail-order businesses also made manufactured items increasingly accessible beyond the cities. And the manufacturers offered items that were appealing because they were new, from clothing fashions to bicycles to folding umbrellas to household appliances. In a society where handmade gifts were common, "store-bought" gifts had the allure of the unusual, a somewhat extravagant luxury that could be seen to represent love even more than handmade gifts. Later, when manufactured gifts became the norm, handmade presents were special, and nostalgia could arise for them as more personal and thoughtful gifts. (And when people purchased gifts instead of making them, they tended to purchase and give more gifts than in the handmade era, a result merchants did not mind at all.)

6. *Commerce had more influence than Christianity in making Christmas the cultur-ally dominant holiday it is in the United States today.* In his book about gift giving in the modern American Christmas, William Waits did not discuss the religious aspects of Christmas. "The reason is simple," he wrote in the introduction:

> Religion has not played an important role in the emergence of the modern form of the celebration. This may come as a surprise—even a shock—to those who think of Christmas as being predominantly religious. However, in practice, the secular aspects of the celebration, such as gift giving, the Christmas dinner, and the gathering of family members, have dwarfed its religious aspects in resources spent and in concern given. Although celebrants may have had meaningful Christmas experiences in church or in other religious settings, they have spent much more time during the holiday season on such secular matters as selecting presents, then wrapping and presenting them, and making arrange-ments for holiday visits and feasts.

If you want to see what is most important to people, he insisted, look at how they spend their time, money, and effort. "One must not confuse the rationale for the celebration," the birthday of Jesus, "with what is central to the celebration as indicated by the behavior of the celebrants."[3]

Waits's argument relates to a point I made in discussing the revival of Christmas in England in the 1800s, after Puritans had effectively deempha-sized Christmas. Christmas came roaring back as a cultural movement. Encouraged by the advocacy and examples of Dickens, Victoria, and Albert, motivated by charity, cultural enjoyment, and commercial interests, it put remarkably minor emphasis on the birth of Jesus. Most Christians happily participated in the Christmas revival, but religious leaders did not drive the cultural resurgence.

As we have already noted, events took a similar path in the United States and England. From a colonial situation in which some Christians celebrated Christmas and others did not, in the nineteenth century Christmas became a thoroughly national pastime in which nearly everyone participated. Again, churches did not push for the expansion, although they may have benefited in church attendance and cultural attention. In the United States the driving force was, more than anyone else, Santa Claus. No longer a saint in a bishop's robes, he was a jolly gift giver who represented magical times, good feeling, and family gatherings, supported by commercial interests. To highlight one phrase by Waits, Santa Claus played a more important role than Christianity "in the emergence of the modern form of the celebration."

7. *Voices of resistance and reform accompanied the rise of a commercialized Christmas throughout the nineteenth and twentieth centuries.* Earlier complaints in American colonial days were about wild behavior, including drunkenness, gaming, obscenities, and general carousing. In the nineteenth and twentieth centuries, when Christmas became more domestic and spending increased, the standard complaint changed to commercialization. Criticisms came from both religious and secular sources, in ministers' sermons, newspaper editorials, voluntary associations for reform, and comments from the general public. For example, the *New York Times* editorialized in 1880, "It seems the fashion to be extravagant, almost reckless, in expenditure, and people of all classes vie with each other in the costliness of their presents until the rivalry in only too many cases becomes nothing more nor less than vulgar ostentation and coarse display of money-bags."[4] Religious voices opposed not only the extravagance but also the displacement of Christian messages. In 1912 the *Sunday School Times* noted,

Merchants have ransacked the earth to find articles to sell, and people have bought lavishly. But commercialism has come in and Christ has been crowded out. There was no room in the inn for the mother of Jesus when the great birthday came. . . . Out of the great bulk of the giving the soul has gone. The day has come to be to many families a burden instead of a delight. Never before was the day so widely or so expensively observed, but its deep and sacred meaning has been too greatly obscured.[5]

In addition to excessive spending and loss of Christian meaning, critics raised concerns about justice, the welfare of workers, and the struggles of the poor. A "Shop Early Campaign" begun in 1906 by the Consumers' League opposed lengthened store hours in the Christmas season, because longer hours would mean that store employees could not spend as much time with their families. The Society for the Prevention of Useless Giving (or SPUG), founded in 1912, campaigned to eliminate the social obligation for workers to buy gifts for their supervisors. Numerous churches organized programs of gifts to the poor at Christmastime.

Criticisms about commercialization continue today, built upon the efforts of many predecessors who tried to combat the trend, and for most reformers it must seem like a losing battle. In spite of all the concern, the general public has clearly embraced much of the abundance and consumerism that mark the current holiday, and the contest between consumerism and reformers lives on.

The developments outlined in these seven generalizations laid the foundation for what happened in the twentieth century and what continues today, especially in the United States. In earlier Christmases gifts were not a major feature. Industrialization brought the production of commodities, and businesses learned that holidays could become occasions to market new products. In the United States gift giving shifted from Saint Nicholas' Day and New Year's Day to Christmas, manufactured gifts replaced handmade goods, and commercial encouragement helped make Christmas an increasingly important holiday in American culture. Today, and all along the way, critics have been concerned about the implications of the commercialization that resulted.

CARDS, DECORATIONS, ☃ AND WRAPPING PAPER ☃

With those generalizations for background, consider some specific examples. Of course, when people refer to the commercialization of Christmas, they usually think of gifts, with good reason, but commerce is involved in many other aspects of the Christmas season as well. To put it crassly, there are a lot of ways you can make money at Christmastime. Three major examples are Christmas cards, home decorations, and (please do not think this is trivial) wrapping paper. Examining these three categories of Christmas products first, before we get to gifts, can help demonstrate how extensive is the commercial activity surrounding Christmas. Notice that all three arose in the 1800s and 1900s, out of a common background of industrialization, the development of consumer culture, and a commodification of the Christmas holiday.

Christmas cards. Apparently the first Christmas card was produced in England by John Calcott Horsley, commissioned by Henry Cole, in 1843. Horsley printed and sold 1,000 copies of a card that featured three drawings side by side. The picture in the center depicted a family seated at a table, and the pictures on either side portrayed examples of helping the poor. Christmas cards did not catch on immediately but began to flourish in England by the 1860s.

The Christmas card custom had several predecessors. New Year's cards (flat cards, not folded) were exchanged in Europe as far back as the 1400s, and Valentine's Day cards of the 1820s preceded Christmas cards in

England. In fact, a number of early English Christmas cards displayed flowers, lace, and leaves that did not seem appropriate to Christmas or winter, because they basically replicated Valentine's card artwork. A tradition of sending personal letters at Christmas and the New Year also preceded Christmas cards, and critics complained that the cards were a poor replacement for the letters, because the brief, printed card messages were not as personal or as substantial as the letters had been.

In the United States Christmas cards appeared at least by the 1850s, but the person generally regarded as the pioneer of American Christmas cards was a German immigrant named Louis Prang, who printed cards from 1875 to 1890. His meticulous printing techniques and the reproductions of fine art on his cards developed an enthusiastic following among the wealthier strata of society. When inexpensive cards imported from Germany undercut his business, after 1890 he concentrated instead on manufacturing art supplies.

The Prang Christmas cards declined in the 1880s for another reason as well, the rise of "gimcracks." Also called "doodads" or "geegaws," gimcracks were inexpensive, impractical gifts of poor quality, such as figurines or jewelry, and in the 1880s they were the first phase of manufactured Christmas gifts exchanged by adults in the United States. They competed with Prang's expensive cards as the favored memento to give to other adults out of respect or affection. Gimcracks were token gifts for family, friends, and broader circles of acquaintances, but eventually even the purchase of inexpensive presents for so many people became a burden in both time and cost. One store owner recalled a time when "the majority of our women customers came into the store with a Christmas list which was literally a yard long."[6] After 1910 people began to drop the gimcrack fad in favor of Christmas cards, which were both more personal and more practical. As a result of this shift, Christmas gifts then tended to become limited to a person's more intimate circle of family and friends, whereas cards could be sent to the longer list of associates and acquaintances. In this "second period" of

American Christmas cards, postgimcrack, the card tradition was adopted by Americans in general, not just the elite. Thereafter the custom of sending Christmas cards has endured undiminished, through the Depression and World War II, to today. According to some estimates, over 75 percent of Americans now send Christmas cards, more than two and one half billion cards per year. (Lately the United States Postal Service has delivered approximately twenty billion letters, packages, and cards each year between Thanksgiving and Christmas.)[7]

Decorations. Another category for Christmas purchases was and is home decoration, including greenery of several kinds, electric lights, and ornaments. Various forms of greenery were displayed in homes, stores, and churches in the United States before the Christmas tree became widely adopted. Mainly, the greenery included mistletoe, holly, and evergreen boughs. Even though some people may have nostalgic recollections of a family stroll in the woods to gather evergreen branches or to cut down a Christmas tree, the main point here is that good old-fashioned entrepreneurial capitalism brought these products to most Americans, especially in urban areas. It was and is a business.

Mistletoe is a parasitic plant that grows on the branches of a variety of trees, but more important, it not only stays green but even bears fruit in winter. Therefore, it obviously was an appropriate symbol of continuing life and hope in the middle of winter, and mistletoe was included in Roman festivals, Celtic beliefs, and Norse mythology. The custom of kissing under the mistletoe apparently developed in England, perhaps in the seventeenth century, for reasons that are now obscure. Some Christians disapproved of mistletoe because of its "scandalous" associations, but it nevertheless became associated with Christmas, as a result of the snowball process in which Christmas picked up the winter customs of various regions as it rolled along. Mistletoe cannot be found in the back yards of most Americans, so to include it among Christmas decorations someone had to bring it to market. In the nineteenth century most mistletoe for American decorations was harvested from apple trees in France and shipped in wooden crates by steamship to the United States, although some was harvested in the American South as well. Another winter plant, holly and its red berries, is somewhat more available for harvest in the United States.

Yet it was the Christmas tree, widely adopted in the United States after the 1850s, that really created an industry. I traced the tree's development, including its association with gifts, in chapter 3. I mention it again in this chapter to remind us that the tree itself became a commodity. Historian Penne Restad reports that as early as 1840 a farmer's wife from Monmouth, New Jersey, brought evergreens to sell in New York City along with hogs and chickens, and New York newspaper ads mentioned Christmas trees as early as 1843.[8] Several sources credit Mark Carr, a logger from upstate New York, as the first vendor to set up a Christmas tree concession in New York City in 1851, paying one dollar to rent the sidewalk space. He was so successful that his rent was one hundred dollars the following year. By 1900 an estimated 20 to 25 percent of Americans had Christmas trees, and President Theodore Roosevelt became concerned about damage to the nation's forests. He temporarily discontinued the custom of a White House Christmas tree, but he eventually relented because the tree was so important to his children and because his main forestry advisor argued that cutting small trees could provide a healthy thinning of the forests. Another mitigating factor was the development of tree farms that raised trees as a renewable crop specifically for the Christmas market. Trees were grown not only in New England forests but also in the upper Midwest and the West. In 2002, 20.8 million Christmas trees were cut throughout the United States, on 21,904 tree farms covering 447,000 acres, bringing an income of over $500 million for the tree farmers.[9]

Then came another product, the artificial Christmas tree. First developed in Germany from green-dyed goose feathers, artificial trees had reached the United States by 1900. Customers liked the one-time expense instead of an annual outlay at escalating costs, and the artificial trees boasted no pine needles, less fire hazard, and perhaps an environmental benefit. The trees may have looked artificial in earlier years, but recent advancements have been so dramatic that manufacturers now market their products by naming the exact tree they imitate, such as Douglas fir or Colorado blue spruce. By 1991, artificial trees began outselling natural trees in the United States.

A related Christmas product was the small, decorative electric light, a welcome replacement for the dangerous custom of lighted candles on trees. The first working electric lights on a Christmas tree were displayed in the home of a vice president of Thomas A. Edison's electric company in the 1880s. After that breakthrough, the advancements came fast and furious.

- in 1901, GE began marketing *individual* working electric lights for Christmas trees
- in 1903, Ever-Ready Company introduced sets of eight lights, wired in a string
- in 1909, GE offered Christmas light bulbs in shapes such as Santas and snowmen
- in the 1920s, cone- or flame-shaped bulbs became available, in addition to the earlier round and pear shapes.
- in 1927, GE introduced parallel wiring that allowed other lights in a series to remain lit when one burned out
- in the 1930s, bubble lights appeared[10]

These examples all refer to Christmas tree lights, but it would be easy to go on and on, citing the more recent explosion of elaborate outdoor Christmas light displays for homes and businesses. Many of those developments occurred in the United States in the post–World War II era, as a part of 1950s suburban life.

The story of decorations also includes ornaments, for the tree and for the home in general. Earlier trees were usually trimmed with candies, wafers, fruit, small presents, and paper ornaments, but the advent of glass ornaments in the 1880s moved more clearly into the commercial arena. The town of Lauscha, in Germany, already known for its glassblowing, invented the glass Christmas ornament and at the beginning was the main supplier for the American market. F. W. Woolworth, founder of the retail chain by the same name, remembered being persuaded to accept some German ornaments for sale and agreeing with "a great deal of indifference," but when they sold out within two days, he made huge orders in following years. Woolworth visited Germany personally in 1890 and placed an order that year for 1,500 gross of the glass ornaments. He also witnessed the horrid labor conditions of many German glass workers, but with his Gilded Age attitudes he did not seem to be especially bothered. It is claimed that a significant portion of Woolworth's personal wealth was made from the sales of glass Christmas ornaments. He also directed that his stores be decorated in ornaments and greenery at Christmastime. "Make the store look different," he is reported to have said. "This is our harvest time. Make it pay."[11]

Wrapping paper. There is one very important additional Christmas commodity, intimately related to the gifts that stood at the center of the Christmas shopping frenzy: wrapping paper. Keep in mind that prior to the 1860s or 1870s, Christmas gift giving was limited mostly to small presents for children, usually left in Christmas stockings or hung on a tree, and some handmade gifts exchanged among adults, virtually none of which were wrapped. In the 1880s, as the purchase of manufactured goods expanded, along came boxes and wrapping paper. A natural outgrowth of the manufacturing process, boxes allowed large quantities of mass-produced products to be stacked neatly and efficiently, in the warehouse, during shipping, and on a store's shelves. A tumble of cloth dolls or cooking pots simply lying in a heap would no longer do. In the last two decades of the nineteenth century, the per capita use of paperboard tripled, and the number of United States workers who made boxes, sometimes in squalid conditions, grew from 718 workers in 1849 to more than 30,000 in 1899.[12]

As boxes became more common, so did wrapping paper. Wrappings in the late nineteenth century were usually white tissue or brown paper, sometimes with a sprig of holly and a gift tag attached. The Dennison Manufacturing Company of Maine and Massachusetts, begun as a box company, became a forerunner in adding other options for wrapping paper, first by importing colored tissue paper from England and then by manufacturing its own specialized products. Joyce Hall, later the founder of Hallmark Cards, added wrapping paper to her production of cards around 1918. The paper became fancier and fancier as the years went on, and in the United States the practice of wrapping gifts has now become almost universal. One survey indicates that 96 percent of all American households wrap their Christmas presents, averaging thirty-seven gifts per home. A single company, American Greetings, reported that it sold 1.7 billion linear feet of Christmas wrapping paper in one year, enough to circle the globe twelve times.[13]

Yet why bother with wrapping paper at all? The explanation of several historians is that in the transition from homemade gifts to manufactured products, wrapping paper helped hide the commercial nature of the gifts. Once you remove the price tag and wrap the present in paper and bows, it can seem more personal and special, as handmade gifts used to be. Thus, wrapping paper serves as an effective marketing technique for merchants trying to encourage sales, and it helps customers feel positive about their purchases.

That may be true, but we should not discount wrapping paper as a mode of personal expression, sometimes chosen with the recipient in mind, and sometimes expressing the personality of the giver. In the words of Karal Ann Marling, who writes about the meanings of material culture, "wrapping is a communicative, expressive act."

Of course, it is easy to dismiss the whole idea of self-expression through packages as another capitalist sham, wherein pseudo-choices come down to Hallmark's Santa wrap or the other guy's version. But the trouble with small pleasures—the giving and the getting of them—is that they are not small, simple matters at all. They are about nuance, aesthetics, time, feelings, memory.[14]

Even if I deliver a present wrapped in the branded paper of a major department store, it still conveys messages about prestige, value, and distinctiveness.

Yet the main reason for wrapping presents, most people would say, is to create anticipation and surprise. For children's gifts in earlier days, Christmas stockings were a form of wrapping, shrouding the present until the child freed it from its cloth container. Also in the days before wrapping paper, parents would keep children out of a room as they decorated a Christmas tree and adorned it with presents, and then they allowed the children to enter, with looks of surprise and wonder. Wrapping a present adds mystery and excitement to the gift, especially when it sits for days before Christmas under the family tree.

The point of highlighting these Christmas-related products is to demonstrate how many commodities became associated with the holiday season, and this is only the beginning of an almost endless list. There are toy trains that circle the base of Christmas trees, elaborate nutcrackers, ceramic miniature Christmas villages, Santa figurines, Coca-Cola Christmas collectibles, and much more.

𝕭 THE MAIN ATTRACTION—GIFTS 𝕭

Statistics indicate that 97 percent of Americans buy Christmas presents. Over the last century and a half, gift giving has clearly taken a dominant place in the holiday celebration. In a survey conducted before the 2005

Christmas holiday period, Americans said they planned to spend $1,564 per household, with $1,042 for gifts. Some estimates claim that Americans spend more than $200 billion annually on Christmas presents. For me, the most striking statistic is this one: 20 percent of all retail goods sold in the United States are Christmas purchases.

One result, not surprisingly, is indebtedness. In the 2004 Christmas shopping season, 59 percent of Americans incurred or acquired credit card debt. It takes approximately four months for the average American to pay off those Christmas purchases, and 14 percent of Americans were still paying off debts from the past Christmas season as the new season approached.[15]

With gift giving as such a massive practice in the Christmas season, why does it happen? Does it arise from the desires and inclinations of the general public, or is it the result of effective manipulation by business interests? In my view, the answer is not as complicated as it seems. It is both. Businesses, such as toy companies and jewelry stores, do all kinds of things to try to market their products and even start new fads, and sometimes it works. But often it does not, in spite of massive expenditures on advertising or clever product placement. Thus, we in the general public obviously are more than mere pawns. We make choices, and businesses rise or fall depending upon what we choose. In Christmas shopping, as in other examples in the marketplace, economic success results from the push and pull of product offerings, marketing initiatives, and consumer choices.

When consumers give or exchange Christmas gifts, I would suggest that, boiling it down, they do so for one of three basic reasons: to express affection; to fulfill social obligations; or to engage in reciprocal trade. The first reason is the one people embrace most gladly, to show their love to family and friends. The second, social obligations, could occur on many levels, from an employer to an employee, or with distant relatives, or between social acquaintances or coworkers. The third, reciprocal trade, might be a subcategory of the second, as another kind of obligation, but here I am thinking of instances in which I give a person a gift simply because I know that person intends to give me one, or because I want to solicit a gift in return. That is the kind of gift exchange that is jokingly called the "Big Swap." All three motivations point to potential needs filled by people when they choose to buy and give gifts.

Yet it is also true that commercial interests can be influential, and we should not be naive about their persuasion and power. The most fascinating illustration for me is the story about President Franklin D. Roosevelt's decision to change the date of Thanksgiving. Americans had celebrated Thanksgiving long before 1863, when Abraham Lincoln declared it a national holiday and designated the last Thursday of November as Thanksgiving. It was not a national law, but all succeeding presidents continued the custom through annual declarations. When Roosevelt became president, his first Thanksgiving in office was a year in which November had five Thursdays, and Thanksgiving fell on November 30, 1933, the very last day of the month. Business leaders, especially representatives of major department stores, asked him to move the date back one week, to extend the Christmas shopping season. Roosevelt declined, but in 1939 Thanksgiving again fell on the last day of the month, and with the nation still struggling with effects of the Depression, this time he changed the date for Thanksgiving to the next to last Thursday, November 23, instead of November 30. The change proved much more controversial than Roosevelt had anticipated. Although the big department stores were pleased, many smaller businesses were not. Complaints came from all directions, including calendar companies whose products were made inaccurate by the belated change, and from persons whose football games or family vacations were disrupted. About half of the states defied Roosevelt and kept their Thanksgiving on November 30, while the other half followed the president's declaration. That meant that some families whose members lived in more than one state could not get together on Thanksgiving because their vacation days did not coincide. The confusion continued for two more years, as Roosevelt again declared Thanksgiving to be the next to last Thursday in November. Finally, in 1941, Congress stepped in and passed a law unifying the national day of Thanksgiving as the *fourth* Thursday of November (instead of the last or the next to last, and thus a compromise of sorts). This is why I find the story fascinating: the president of the United States changed the traditional day of Thanksgiving, at the request of department store representatives, for one and only one reason—to lengthen the Christmas shopping season.[16]

These brief reflections on gift-giving motivations, and the Thanksgiving example of business influence, make a simple point. The massive spending that now characterizes the American Christmas season is not just the consequence of mercantile encouragement or manipulation. Nor is it simply a spontaneous expression of affection and social obligations among people. The modern commercialized Christmas has resulted from an interplay of both.

⚡ CHRISTMAS MUSIC AND MOVIES ⚡

Two other favorite features of Christmas are music and movies. As most of us do, I have my favorite Christmas songs that I love to sing or hear every year, and there are a couple of classic Christmas movies that I make a ritual of watching annually. We do not usually think of them as products too, but they are. Discount stores feature entire racks of Christmas music CDs, plus videotapes and DVDs of popular movies and classic television programs for the Christmas season. Television and radio stations flood the airwaves with the music and movies as well, brought to us by commercial sponsors. Thus, on one level they are additional examples of saleable products. Yet in addition, an examination of the music lyrics and movie story lines reveals larger themes, reflecting transitions that the American

Christmas has undergone, away from a focus on the nativity story to a more generalized cultural holiday.

Christmas Music. Surveying the wide variety of vocal music that has arisen in association with Christmas, we might cluster the examples into three general categories: traditional hymns, widely known folk songs or carols, and commercially produced popular music. All three categories blur into one another, but the provisional grouping helps us think about the different kinds of music we hear in the Christmas season.

For the category of *traditional hymns* I have in mind many of the historical Christmas hymns of the Christian church, written by monks, theologians, and classical composers over the years. Virtually every Christmas hymn emphasizes the nativity of Jesus and its theological significance, and almost all of them are products of the church. These hymns are sung or performed in church services, but they are generally not the music average Christians know by heart. One of the first such hymns was written by Bishop Ambrose of Milan (339–397), "Veni redemptor gentium" (redeemer of the nations come). In most church hymnals, if you look in the section that contains Christmas hymns it is likely that you will see many that are not familiar to you, composed in medieval, Reformation, or more modern periods. There exists a wealth of such music.

I would like to call the second category *Christmas carols,* but historians and musicologists do not agree on the definition of a Christmas carol. Some use the phrase to refer to all Christmas vocal music, while others prefer to limit it to widely known tunes and lyrics with a religious focus, somewhat closer to folk songs. I prefer the more limited definition. Here I think of the kind of songs that high school church youth groups sing when they go caroling down the sidewalks, stopping at the homes of elderly citizens who are homebound. Most of the carols are not really folk songs, because their composers and authors are known, but these are the favorite, familiar religious songs that people like to sing, such as "Joy to the World,"

"Silent Night," "O Little Town of Bethlehem," and "It Came Upon a Midnight Clear."

A third kind of Christmas music has developed as well, especially within the last century, and some of the songs have become so familiar that church carolers often sing them too. They are songs composed for commercial purposes, recorded for sale by popular artists, and they usually focus on the cultural aspects of Christmas rather than the nativity story or its meaning. This is what I would call *commercially produced popular Christmas music.* Think of "I Saw Mommy Kissing Santa Claus," or "Jingle Bell Rock." If you examine the store racks featuring CDs of Christmas music today, they will include some CDs with a sacred focus and some with a few religious songs mixed in among commercial secular songs, but the vast majority of the selections, in jazz, country, rock, and a wide range of other styles, are songs about the cultural experience of Christmas.

Among the seemingly endless examples in this popular commercial category, which ones have been the most successful in American culture? The two that are usually claimed to be the best-selling Christmas recordings of all time are "Rudolph the Red-Nosed Reindeer," in second place, and "White Christmas" in first. Both have interesting background stories.

Rudolph the red-nosed reindeer appeared initially in a poem published as a children's book and then became the subject of a song. Many Christmas traditions develop as folkways over a long period, but Rudolph was a phenomenon that emerged virtually overnight and quickly took its place in the enduring Santa Claus mythology. Christmas historian Gerry Bowler has called it "one of the great marketing coups of all time."[17] Robert May worked for the advertising department of Montgomery Ward, a department store and mail-order business, and he was asked to write an animal story to be given away as a Christmas promotion. The result was the poem "Rudolph the Red-Nosed Reindeer," with art by Denver Gillen, and Montgomery Ward distributed almost two and one half million copies of the booklet in 1939. In 1946 the company decided to produce and distribute it again, this time three and a half million copies, and then generously turned over the rights to May. The poem became a commercially published book, and May's brother-in-law, Johnny Marks, wrote a song that summarized the Rudolph story. They tried to convince Bing Crosby, Dinah Shore, and others to record the song but were turned down. Finally Gene Autry, the singing cowboy, agreed, and audience enthusiasm at his concerts convinced his record company to feature the song, which sold two million recordings in 1949 alone. The rest, as they say, is history. The poem has been translated into over twenty-five languages, the song has been recorded by more artists than I can count, and a 1964 animated cartoon narrated by Burl Ives has become an annual television classic.

Many people have aspired to the same success by producing their own Christmas songs, characters, poems, and stories, and most of them have failed. Why did this poem and song touch such a chord with the American public? First, it associated itself with the already popular "Night Before Christmas" poem by elaborating upon the characters of Santa and his reindeer, using a similar rhyme structure, and even ending with a similar line, "Happy Christmas to all, and to all a good-night." Second, Rudolph's story connects with every child or adult who has experienced teasing and rejection. The song and poem tell the story of a reindeer who was ridiculed by his peers because of his shiny red nose, but after his nose provided light for Santa Claus and his sleigh on a foggy Christmas Eve, Rudolph was praised by Santa and envied by the other reindeer. It is the kind of vindication we all wish we had. Third, the song had the advantage of prior commercial promotion of the Rudolph story through the millions of booklets distributed by Montgomery Ward.

Even Rudolph, however, pales in comparison to the best-selling Christmas song of all time, "White Christmas." Irving Berlin already was an established composer of hits, starting with "Alexander's Ragtime Band" in 1911, and he later composed such standards as "Blue Skies," "Puttin' on the Ritz," "God Bless America," "There's No Business Like Show

Business," "Easter Parade," and many more, with a total production of more than 1,500 songs. Yet his most famous song by far was "White Christmas," with sales that amazed even Berlin, who famously called it "the greatest song anybody ever wrote."

In 1938 Twentieth Century-Fox had produced the movie *Alexander's Ragtime Band* as a vehicle to include twenty-three Berlin compositions. In 1942 Paramount decided it wanted to do something similar, and since Berlin had already written many songs about holidays, he was the one who came up with the idea for the movie *Holiday Inn*, a romantic comedy and musical in which the song and dance team of Bing Crosby and Fred Astaire turned an inn into a special nightclub only eight nights a year for special holiday performances. Many of the musical numbers already were familiar hits, but Berlin composed "White Christmas" especially for this film. He won an Oscar for the song, the only Academy Award Berlin ever received, and Bing Crosby adopted it as his unofficial theme song. Crosby sang "White Christmas" again in the movie *Blue Skies* (1946), and a third time in *White Christmas* (1954), where the very name of the film tried to cash in on the song's popularity. Bing Crosby's original Decca version of the song sold over 31 million copies, standing "for over fifty years . . . as the best-selling record in history," unseated from its place in the *Guinness Book of World Records* only by Elton John's tribute to Princess Diana, "Candle in the Wind '97." Sales of "White Christmas" in its many versions are more than 125 million. Jody Rosen, who has written a book about Berlin and his song, adds,

> "White Christmas" is the biggest pop tune of all time, the top-selling and most frequently recorded song: the hit of hits. It is a quintessentially American song that the world has embraced; among the untold hundreds of "White Christmas" recordings are versions in Dutch, Hungarian, Japanese, Swahili, and, in a knowing nod to its creator's pedigree, Yiddish.[18]

One reason for the song's initial success was the context of World War II, and for soldiers far away from home the melancholy, nostalgic composition became an "anthem for homesickness" (along with "I'll be Home for Christmas"). Yet the popularity carried on long after the war, continuing to resonate with the desires of many for an idealized, snowy Christmas. It appeals to almost everyone. While some find it ironic that a Jewish composer wrote the most popular Christmas song, Berlin's composition contains no explicitly religious references and draws instead upon the holiday as winter festival, which can include all celebrants regardless of religious belief. Berlin was successful because he knew how to appeal to the general public. "A good song embodies the feelings of the mob," he said. "A songwriter is not much more than a mirror which reflects those feelings."[19]

Christmas Movies. Berlin's "White Christmas" has already led us into the realm of Christmas movies. Everyone seems to have his or her own favorites, from classics like *Meet Me in St. Louis* to modern comedies such as *National Lampoon's Christmas Vacation* and *The Santa Clause.* Christmas movies cover the entire history of cinema, from silent films to today. In 1913, during the era of silent movies, *Moving Picture World* published an editorial that proclaimed,

> Christmas is the picture season of the year. . . . A generation ago a Christmas entertainment without the Christmas tree and stereopticon was not only incomplete but lacking in true, attractive, and instructive power. We have grown with the times. . . . How tremendously the moving picture helps and enlarges the Christmas opportunities. What great pictures are now ready. Never such pictures. Never such projection.

The editorial writer saw in the Christmas season both business opportunities for film exhibitors and a chance to serve the needs of churches, children, and the poor with free showings. "Make the season and the entertainment harmonize; it increases your profit and reputation; it pleases and educates; it gives greater satisfaction and the remembrances are pleasant ones."[20]

Of the Christmas movies produced since those days, few focus mainly on the birth story of Jesus, although the birth has been included in most larger Jesus movies, such as *The Greatest Story Ever Told* (1965) or *Jesus of Nazareth* (1977). *Three Godfathers* (1948), a western, had a plot that was a clear Christmas allegory. The movie has been remade several times, and each version comes about as close to a nativity-centered Christmas movie as I can imagine. The other exception is *Come to the Stable* (1949), a movie that faced many obstacles because it was reportedly too religious. Other than that, Christmas movies represent a wide variety of styles and subject matter, including numerous versions of Dickens's *Christmas Carol,* horror movies with a Christmas setting, comedies, touching family movies, and more.

One measure of the most popular Christmas movies might be the number of times television stations air them during the Christmas season. By that measure, three movies stand out: *It's a Wonderful Life* (1946), *Miracle on 34th Street* (1947, with additional remakes), and *A Christmas Story* (1983).

It's a Wonderful Life was a box-office disappointment when it was first released, but in the 1970s it slipped into the public domain, which meant that television stations could show it repeatedly without paying royalties. The resulting exposure developed a wide, devoted audience that now regards the movie as the great American Christmas story. It is a touching tale of a man contemplating suicide who is transformed with the help of his family, friends, and a bumbling angel.

Miracle on 34th Street centers on a character who actually thinks he is Santa Claus. It is "a joyful and moving story about goodness and faith and our human need for fantasy," and it also highlights a little girl's desire for a family and a home.[21] Praised for its balance of whimsy and touching moments, the movie won three Academy Awards. I admit that I am one of those persons who find the Christmas season incomplete until I arrange time for an annual viewing.

A Christmas Story is the rare movie that has broken through to become a modern classic. You will note that the previous two movies were made in the 1940s, along with other standards like *Holiday Inn* and *Meet Me in St. Louis*. Hosts of viewers now rank *A Christmas Story* with or above those older classics. It is a hilarious family comedy focused on a boy, Ralphie Parker, who is totally obsessed with receiving an air rifle for Christmas, a Genuine Red Ryder Carbine-Action Two Hundred–Shot Lightning Loader Range Model Air Rifle with a Shock-Proof High Adventure Combination Trail Compass and Sundial set in the stock. (I laugh every time I read the description of the rifle. If you have seen the movie, you will understand.)

Do you notice any common themes in all of these examples of Christmas music and movies? First of all, of course, the songs and movies are all commodities, commercially produced for the Christmas season. Four of the five feature gifts as important to Christmas, with the possible exception of "White Christmas." Although they are Christmas favorites, both songs and all three movies have virtually nothing to do with a baby Jesus in a manger. All five are moving or heartwarming, affirming values that are widely appreciated in American society. And four of the five have winter settings, although *Miracle on 34th Street* might be considered deficient in snow.

Just as Irving Berlin likened the songwriter to a mirror that reflects "the feelings of the mob," I contend that these examples of popular culture—songs and movies embraced by so many fans—reflect what the American Christmas has become. As seen in this mirror, Christmas is a culturewide celebration of traditional values, family, and good feelings, set in the middle of winter. With few explicit references to Christian teachings or doctrine, it is mostly a cultural winter festival, thus inclusive of people of many backgrounds. It is not necessarily anti-Christian, and many Christians who love the songs and movies feel fully comfortable participating in the cultural winter festival and at the same time affirming their beliefs in Jesus as incarnation, God with us. And yes, as seen in the mirror of popular culture, shopping and gifts have become central parts of the Christmas experience.

six

WRESTLING

WITH

CHRISTMAS

In one of the memorable stories in the book of Genesis, scripture for Jews and Christians alike, Jacob wrestled all night long with a mysterious adversary who resisted identification. When morning came, neither side had prevailed, but Jacob came away from the encounter with a limp and a blessing (Genesis 32:22–32). Jacob's wrestling serves as a resonant image for me when I grapple with many issues, reminding me that the struggles can be long and draining and the challenges unclear, but there is hope about the outcome. I think that applies to wrestling with Christmas.

For many of us, Christmas is a beloved season of the year, but it is mixed with frustrations. Those frustrations are of several kinds, but for most of my life they were simply jumbled together. As much as I enjoyed Christmas, I also had a sense that it could be more meaningful and fulfilling but somehow never took the time to diagnose my dissatisfactions. Yet the more I learned about the history of Christmas, and the more I have talked with audiences and close friends, three issues have begun to crystallize for me. This list is not exhaustive, but three issues come up again and again.

When I ask people what they would like to change about Christmas, some say they wish the holiday were more spiritually meaningful. Some say they want to escape the spending pressures and the hectic pace of the season. Some wonder, in a pluralistic nation and world, what is the best way for people who feel like "outsiders"—their friends of other religions, or of no religion at all—to find common ground at Christmastime. And some worry about all three topics, recognizing that they often intermingle. I have no pretensions about being able to offer magic solutions for any of them, but I would like to briefly consider each one in turn. Does this book's historical summary provide any helpful perspectives?

✁ SPIRITUAL MESSAGES OF CHRISTMAS ✁

One concern about Christmas comes from Christians who fear that the spiritual meanings of the season get lost in the midst of so many cultural symbols and activities. They express their misgivings in two distinct ways. On one hand, a number of Christians are introspective and self-critical, asking themselves if they have become so preoccupied with decorations, gifts, and dinner preparations that they have forgotten "the reason for the season," the birth of Jesus. On the other hand, some Christians complain about public actions and displays at Christmastime that do not acknowledge Christianity or Jesus. For instance, they may get upset over department store signs that read "Happy Holidays" instead of "Merry Christmas," claiming that it is anti-Christian to cash in on Christmas without reference to the holiday's Christian basis. In other words, one concern is about whether *my own personal* Christmas observances are Christian enough, and the other concern is about whether *society's* Christmas observances are Christian enough. Campaigns to "Keep Christ in Christmas" might refer to either one of these concerns, or both. It pertains to what people call the secularization of Christmas.

This issue, obviously, is of special importance for Christians, because they (or we) value and do not want to lose the spiritual dimensions of the holiday; the next portion of this chapter, about commercialization and stress, is relevant not only to people who identify themselves as Christian but to lots of other people too. Yet on this topic of secularization, much of the conversation is Christian to Christian, and I identify myself as part of the circle. I am a college religious studies professor, an active United Methodist, and Christmas is one of my favorite times of the year, so I personally wrestle with these issues along with other Christians. Because I share that background, let me audaciously offer some comments as one Christian to other Christians who struggle with challenges about spiritual aspects of the season. Based on the history summarized here, I believe we first need to face two facts.

Fact number 1. There never was a pure spiritual Christmas. When Christmas started in the fourth century, right in the middle of three Roman winter festivals, it was, from its very first moments, a winter party with Christian meanings added on top. Even in the early years many participants wanted mainly to have fun and let loose. Bill McKibben, who wrote a little book to encourage more meaningful Christmases, recognized this in the clever title of his first chapter, "Christmas Never Was Christmas." We human beings have a tendency to create golden ages of the past, when all was supposedly wonderful before complicating factors intruded and ruined everything. In most cases, the golden age is an idealized dream: the actual Christmas that early Christians experienced was both a boisterous seasonal party and a religiously meaningful observance. Both.

Fact number 2. Today, some people who really enjoy Christmas are not especially interested in its religious aspects. That is just the way it is. I've already mentioned the most dramatic example for me, the existence of Christmas in Japan. Stores and public spaces in Japan feature lights and other decorations, a vast majority of Japanese homes have Christmas trees, friends send Christmas cards to one another, romantic couples exchange gifts, and children excitedly await presents that Santa Claus will bring on Christmas Eve. When I ask Japanese friends about this, they confirm it all, and then they quickly add, "but for us it's not religious." In a country where less than 2 percent of the population is Christian, Christmas in Japan clearly is a cultural rather than a religious celebration. The Japanese example also reminds me of a Chinese American family who once lived in an apartment above mine. They were nominally Buddhist, but they had a Christmas tree, exchanged presents, and thoroughly enjoyed the season.

Of course, a number of other Americans are the same way. I know several white, middle-class, midwestern families who throw themselves fully into Christmas festivities and have huge dinners on Christmas day with all their relatives, but they have not attended church for years and do not intend to. They might hold various personal religious views, but the basic reality is that they do not think much about religion or spiritual beliefs during the Christmas season. Yet they like Christmas.

Indeed, there are two Christmases: a cultural Christmas, and a religious or Christian Christmas. Some people focus on one, some focus on the other, and many are involved in both. In the modern United States, the cultural Christmas includes features such as evergreen decorations, Santa Claus, songs like "White Christmas," and holiday shopping. The religious or Christian Christmas includes church services, Christmas Bible stories from Matthew and Luke, hymns like "Away in the Manger," and messages about God with us, and love, joy, and peace. The vast majority of Christians experience both kinds of Christmas fully intertwined in their lives, seeing it all as one.

Because of the popularity of the cultural Christmas, Christians have begun to recognize that the holiday is not fully in their control. We cannot claim that it is "no longer" controlled by Christians, because it never was, fully. To say it again, winter festivals preexisted Christianity and later merged with an observance of Jesus' birthday, and winter parties still continue as important human experiences in their own right, important for both Christians and non-Christians. It gets complicated, because winter and Christian terms cross over at times and become associated with practices beyond their original meanings. For example, the pre-Christian "Yule" has become a term to designate Christmas, and "Christmas" has become a term to designate winter activities.

Given this mixed heritage, it seems foolish of Christians to become angry when others choose to embrace the winter festivity but do not get involved in the religious part. It is their choice. Am I supposed to be upset with the Japanese Christmas and tell them to stop it? If a person says "Happy Holidays" or "Season's Greetings," isn't it a simple acknowledgment that lots of people enjoy midwinter parties for lots of different reasons? When I understand the elementary human appeal of lights and feasting in a season of cold and depression, it helps me loosen up a bit about all of this celebrating, as a good and natural thing for human beings of many backgrounds to do, including, yes, even Christians.

In light of this same history, I do not support those who complain that American society does not recognize Christmas enough in its public symbols and activities. Think back to the colonial era and the early nation. Christians did not agree with other Christians on the importance of Christmas. Those from denominations that valued Christmas were free to celebrate it in the most meaningful ways they could, but in the overall society life went on as usual, many businesses remained open, public schools were in session, and Congress even met on Christmas Day. Some devout folks think things were better back then, because Christians might have been more spiritually intent on observing Christmas, instead of doing it just for social reasons. Then and now, Christians in the United States can observe Christmas if they choose. And if they wish to be public about it, they can place explicitly Christian displays on their own lawn or in front of churches. Is it the role of businesses or governments to become active promoters of the religious aspect of the holiday? Why would Christians even expect it?

Yet I am very sympathetic with religious groups and individual Christians who hope to keep a vital spiritual center in their own Christmas celebrations. It is good to be introspective and examine our own lives, and I recognize that if I neglect to give much attention during the Christmas season to the birth of Jesus and its meaning, the main responsibility for the problem rests with me. Admittedly, I can resolve to find time for daily devotions, or attend church more regularly, or develop some family Advent traditions, but with all of the other pressures of the season, it is not easy. To give more attention to the spiritual meanings of Christmas, are there any special, creative ideas or strategies that might help?

One idea I do not recommend is to start a campaign to turn Christmas into the purely spiritual holiday it never was. My understanding is that the Christmas message is "incarnation," that God entered fully into the world in the birth of Jesus. So combining Jesus' birthday party with at least some worldly celebrating seems appropriate.

However, I have encountered three other ideas that are intriguing, or even a little "outside the box." The first one is mainly meant to be provocative, but maybe all three could fuel your own brainstorming process.

Eliminate Christmas. I doubt that this will be a very popular option, but it is, after all, what the Puritans tried to do. Lest today's Christians distance themselves from the Puritans by considering them just an odd group of people, an aberration from the past, remember that in the United States they were a mainstream denomination called Congregationalists, and Presbyterians, Baptists, Quakers, and Methodists joined them in deemphasizing or eliminating the observance of Christmas. In remembrance of the Puritans, ask yourself what would be gained and what would be lost if you stopped celebrating Christmas. It was an option attempted by a significant portion of the American colonial population, although the opposition to Christmas faded away over time. Today, Jehovah's Witnesses and a few other unconventional groups arising from Christianity also choose not to celebrate Christmas, for varying reasons.

One iconoclastic evangelical Christian writer, Rodney Clapp, almost seems to endorse this option in a short essay titled "Let the Pagans Have Their Holiday." Christmas has overtaken Easter in popular observances and popular piety, he notes, but rather than drop Christmas Clapp wants

Christians to return to "seeing Easter as the main Christian holiday." He argues, "surely Easter, and not the Christmas on which we modern Western Christians focus most of our attention, is the 'fulcrum that balances Christian life.' Christmas celebrated without the events of Easter overshadowing is too easily sentimentalized and secularized." Clapp wants to "return Easter to its rightful prominence."[1]

Embrace the cultural Christmas as a gift to the Christ child. Earl Count, an Episcopal priest and anthropology professor, wrote a tiny book about Christmas that touched upon pre-Christian influences and mentioned many traditions that were added to Christmas over the years, especially in northern Europe. Instead of being bothered by the addition of so many traditions, some more related to Jesus than others, he viewed them all as a popular response to the Christmas story. Count summarizes the idea in these words:

> Christmas is a spontaneous drama of the common folk, a prayer, a hymn. All the while that Raphael was painting the Sistine Madonna, Frenchmen building the cathedral of Chartres, English bishops composing the *Book of Common Prayer,* Handel his *Messiah,* Bach his *B-Minor Mass,* the common people, out of whom these geniuses sprang, were composing Christmas.[2]

Thus, he views customs of the cultural Christmas—built up as the snowball rolled through Europe and elsewhere—as gifts that the masses bring to the manger of the Christ child. If we took Count's approach, we might be more relaxed and comfortable with the many aspects of celebration, as a "spontaneous" response to the birth of Jesus into the world.

Revive the twelve days of Christmas as a time for religious focus. For the United States culture at large, much of the hubbub of Christmas stops dead on December 26. It normally starts on the day after Thanksgiving (or increasingly, even earlier), with a dizzying array of activities: shopping, decorating the house inside and out, writing a Christmas letter and sending

Christmas cards, planning and participating in Christmas parties, attending seasonal plays and concerts, preparing food, and more. Then, except for the rush of gift returns and exchanges, Christmas is suddenly over. Radio stations that had broadcast Christmas music twenty-four hours a day since Thanksgiving change the format at midnight on Christmas Day, or even earlier. Discarded Christmas trees start appearing beside trash containers on December 26.

If an individual, a family, or a congregation chooses the twelve days of Christmas as a time for spiritual emphasis, there will be almost no competition, except for the flurry of energy on New Year's Eve and Day. Instead of a post-Christmas letdown, the twelve days between Christmas and Epiphany could be an amazingly peaceful time, for daily devotions on the meaning of Christmas, special family commitments and activities, and church-sponsored reflections. Imagine it, twelve days free for spiritual purposes. I personally like this idea. Make the twelve days of Christmas a time of spiritual focus, when it is less likely that the clatter of surrounding activities will drown out reflections on the birth of the Christ child.

Your ideas?

❧ COMMERCIALIZATION AND STRESS ❧

As I have noted, for many Christians concern about spiritual meanings at Christmastime and frustrations about commercialization and stress are all bound together, because shopping and hectic schedules often swamp religious reflection. Yet it may be helpful to separate the two. Celebrants who are not especially religious still seek a less hectic and more fulfilling Christmas. Also, addressing one issue does not always automatically solve the other.

When frustrated folks seek solutions for both commercialization and stress, they usually try to "simplify Christmas." Standing in a long tradition of Christmas reformers, groups interested in voluntary simplicity arose several decades ago as part of a countercultural yearning for environmental protection, peace, and justice. Others became interested in simplifying Christmas simply because of their personal dissatisfactions with the Christmas holiday. Bill McKibben, a participant in this movement, offered this description of the problem:

> Christmas had become something to endure at least as much as it had become something to enjoy—something to dread at least as much as something to look forward to. Instead of an island of peace amid a busy life, it was an island of bustle. The people we were talking to wanted so much more out of Christmas: more music, more companionship, more contemplation, more time outdoors, more love. And they realized that to get it, they needed less of some other things: not so many gifts, not so many obligatory parties, not so much hustle.[3]

Does any of this sound familiar?

Various resources are now available for simplifying Christmas, and it strikes me that they all have some very common themes. One is simply the need to get off autopilot. For many of us, when Christmas approaches we simply slide into responding to the numerous obligations of the season: planning and attending parties, sending cards, decorating the home, buying gifts, and on down the racetrack. If we want things to change, we have to take time before the season starts, alone or with family and friends, to *choose* what kind of Christmas we want instead of just letting it happen to us. The secret is to be intentional, not just reactive. And that takes some conscious decision making at the beginning.

Thus, it is helpful to go through a deliberate self-examination process, to summarize what we have done in the past, decide in general what we value, and then apply our values to the list of past activities and choose which ones should continue and which ones might change. Each step takes a little time, and each step may bring unexpected revelations. I have helped lead a few workshops based on the book *Unplug the Christmas Machine* (described below), and when participants filled out surveys for themselves about their past practices, most people expressed surprise about one thing or another. One husband said that, until now, he did not realize that his wife was responsible for almost all of the Christmas tasks, which seemed unfair. Another participant thought that she spent most of her money on gifts, and she was amazed to learn that she spent so much on other Christmas expenses like postage, decorations, food, and more. A systematic assessment is very helpful.

I do not believe that it is wise to impose one notion or model of an ideal Christmas upon everyone, because it depends on the needs and values of each person. In the words of Bill McKibben, "There is no ideal Christmas, only the Christmas you decide to make as a reflection of your values, desires, affections, traditions."[4]

Another common theme is this: As we try to figure out what we want or need for Christmas, we should look below the surface. "The issue is not the issue" is a standard aphorism for some counselors. At times a client will walk into a counselor's office complaining about a problem, but conversation reveals that it is really a symptom of a deeper problem. Applied to Christmas, when asked what we want for Christmas the temptation is to provide a gift list, but in fact what really matters is something else, like sharing love with family and friends, or finding time to be refreshed. One of the books on this topic discusses "four things children really want for Christmas," calling them four basic needs: a relaxed and loving time with family; realistic expectations about gifts; an evenly paced holiday season; and reliable family traditions.[5]

A list like this highlights deeper needs than our superficial material desires, and adults probably need to clarify the same kind of list for themselves. The process also can help us clarify and/or remind ourselves of our basic values.

Unplug the Christmas Machine, by Jo Robinson and Jean Coppock Staeheli, has become almost an unofficial Bible for persons interested in simplifying Christmas. I avoided this book for a long time, because from the title I assumed that the authors wanted to make me feel guilty about sending out too many Christmas cards, or about wasting money on Christmas lights. In addition, if they were anti-Christmas I did not want to hear it, because I like Christmas. However, Robinson and Staeheli are not against Christmas; they *are* against the Christmas *machine.* The book is a reasonable, sensitive, and very practical discussion of many struggles people have with Christmas, based upon conversations and workshops they have conducted for years. Robinson and Staeheli's discussion is influenced by an underlying philosophy, summarized in their Christmas Pledge:

> Believing in the true spirit of Christmas, I commit myself to
>
> - Remember those people who truly need my gifts
> - Express my love in more direct ways than gifts
> - Examine my holiday activities in the light of my deepest values
> - Be a peacemaker within my circle of family and friends
> - Rededicate myself to my spiritual growth[6]

Among several other resources on simplifying Christmas, one book I would mention is *Hundred Dollar Holiday: The Case for a More Joyful Christmas,* by Bill McKibben. It arose from a program McKibben led some years ago among rural United Methodist churches in upper New York state. McKibben, a former staff writer for the *New Yorker,* had the idea that setting a limit on the money spent for Christmas would help people turn their attention to other priorities, although there was nothing magical about the number he chose (he liked the alliteration with "holiday"). This is a tiny book, almost a pamphlet, that summarizes a philosophy for a more simple and joyful

Christmas without giving many specific suggestions. One stimulating insight that McKibben proposes is this: what we need from Christmas has changed since the era of the late 1800s when the modern American Christmas developed. Then, in a culture of scarcity, gifts were very special, and then, in the isolation of rural America, hustle and bustle broke the monotony. Now, says McKibben, we have so many possessions that "we are—in nearly every sense of the word—stuffed. Saturated. Trying to cram in a little more on December 25 seems kind of pointless."[7] Further, in today's hectic life, a holiday of peace and quiet would be more special than numerous activities. Because our situation has changed, what would make Christmas special also has changed, McKibben says.

❧ CHRISTMAS AND "OUTSIDERS" ❧

How persons of other religions or no religion relate to a culturally dominant Christmas is an increasingly contentious issue in American society. Many disputes have involved legal and public policy issues, such as nativity scenes on the steps of county courthouses, or public high school choirs singing Christmas music. The First Amendment issues are important, but here I am more interested in interpersonal relationships. What is it like for a Jew or a Buddhist to live through a Christmas season in the United States? Is it appropriate to send a Christmas card to a nonreligious friend? Do we all have to walk on eggshells?

Millions of people do not identify themselves as Christian. Tom Flynn is one. An ex-Catholic who is now an atheist, he has written about the "old outsiders" and the "new outsiders" in American culture. The old outsiders are Jews and the nonreligious; both groups have had a long history in the United States. From perhaps five thousand Jews in the United States in 1850, there were about two and one half million by 1924, and there are about five and one half million today. This total includes both those who

identify themselves religiously and ethnically. Flynn's general category of
nonreligious reaches as far back as the deists in colonial America, people
who today may call themselves atheists, agnostics, rationalists, freethinkers,
or secular humanists. The size of this group is very unclear, but if you
include those who answer surveys as atheist, agnostic, or no religious preference, it may be 11 percent of the population, over twenty-eight million
people (though "no religious preference" might include people who are
vaguely Christian but not affiliated with a particular institutional group).
By another measure, if 94 percent of Americans believe in God, that would
seem to mean that 6 percent do not, which would be over fifteen million
people. The new outsiders Flynn discusses include "America's religious non-
Judaeo-Christians: Muslims, Hindus, Buddhists, Confucianists, Shintos,
Baha'is, Sikhs, adherents of Native American religions, Wiccans, and
more." They are new because many were more recent immigrants. One
source numbers them at 5 percent of the population, or almost thirteen
million members.[8]

The point is that these groups include millions and millions of people.
Yet they are, indeed, a minority when compared with the number who call
themselves Christian. Several of my non-Christian friends tell me that the
Christmas season is the time of year when they feel most like outsiders, on
the margins of American life. In the words of Rabbi Lawrence Hoffman,
it is like slipping "into the role of a visitor to a foreign culture." If some
Christians claim that all specific identifications of Christmas are being
removed from the holiday season, they have not looked at the cultural
context through the eyes of an outsider. As described by Rabbi Hoffman,

> It was, and still is, no picnic explaining to your children that Jews don't
> celebrate Christmas. They stare at you in disbelief. Everyone keeps Christmas,
> they plead. It is the topic of every television program, the display in every store
> window. The Radio City Music Hall features its annual Christmas spectacle
> and the Metropolitan Museum of Art displays Christmas artifacts. What do

you mean? We don't celebrate Christmas? Does that make us the Grinch? Maybe Scrooge?[9]

Jews call this the December dilemma. Taking American Jews as an example of the many outsiders, what choices do they have in responding to the Christmas season? Logically, there seem to be three.

One option is to accommodate to the larger culture, participating in the symbols and the customs of the season. That could include a home Christmas tree and gift exchanges. One rationale for this option would be to treat these activities as a cultural but not necessarily a religious observance, and indeed, the history summarized in this book might make that case. Before the 1930s in Germany, a number of prominent Jewish families had Christmas trees in their homes, justifying them as German customs rather than as Christian. Another argument for this choice could be that the cultural spirit of the season includes generosity and concern for the poor, values fully consistent with Judaism.

An opposite option is to reject any participation in Christmas. In the words of one rabbi, "Notwithstanding the commercialization and secularization of the holiday, it [Christmas] remains a deeply Christian celebration, and, as such, has no place in the home life of a Jewish family."[10] Faculty members at some Jewish seminaries have been expected to keep office hours on Christmas Day, and some Jewish businesses remain open.

In between, as a third option, would be various compromises, maintaining Jewish identity but participating in more innocuous activities of the season. Even the observance of Hanukkah, or Chanukah, may be a compromise of a sort, because it was a minor Jewish holiday expanded in order to provide, essentially, a Jewish substitute for Christmas. An increased emphasis on children and gifts during Hanukkah clearly bears a resemblance to the American Christmas.

I do not know if this qualifies as a compromise under the third option, but an inspiring example of Jewish actions at Christmastime occurs when

Jews volunteer to take the place of Christians scheduled to work on Christmas Day, so that the Christians can celebrate Christmas with their families. It has been arranged on an individual basis and at times as part of an organized Jewish volunteer effort, to cover for hospital and nursing home workers, in various civic services, and wherever else workers are needed.

I am in no position to advise Jews, or any other non-Christians, what path they should choose at Christmastime in negotiating their way through the dominant culture. I do wish that people in my camp, the Christians, would spend more time trying to sympathetically understand what it is like to be an outsider during the Christmas season.

And I have one other thought about how people of different religions and cultures might relate to one another in the month of December. Maybe we should return to the subject with which this book began, winter. Despite religious diversity, and some secularism, in most parts of Europe and North America we all share the experience of winter. Our thermostats and electric lights may make it easier to endure in the modern era, but winter remains a challenge. It tests us as it brings darkness, depression, and danger, and we need light and inspiration to lift our spirits. If we are going to find any December commonality, it might be there.

I am not suggesting that Christmas is religiously neutral and thus, that all groups should unify around Christmas as common ground. Neither am I advocating the invention of yet another winter festival to bring religions together. I do suggest that we look at each other's December celebrations to see what they have in common. Christmas's roots in a midwinter celebration present not so much a problem but a path to a solution, if persons from different religions and cultures can appreciate their common human impulse to celebrate and survive, to search for joy and meaning, in the middle of winter.

NOTES

ONE FIRST THERE WAS WINTER

1. Clement A. Miles, *Christmas Customs and Traditions: Their History and Significance* (New York: Dover Publications, 1976), 173; first published in 1912, under a different title.

2. Stephen Nissenbaum, *The Battle for Christmas* (New York: Alfred A. Knopf, 1996), 5–6.

3. Simon Hornblower and Antony Spawforth, eds., *The Oxford Classical Dictionary*, 3rd ed., s.v. "Saturnalia."

4. Tanya Gulevich, *Encyclopedia of Christmas* (Detroit: Omnigraphics, 2000), 556.

5. Lucian, *Lucian VI*, trans. K. Kilburn, Loeb Classical Library (Cambridge, MA: Harvard University Press, 1959), 107, 113, 115.

6. Lucian, *Lucian VI*, 93.

7. Lucian, *Lucian VI*, 91.

8. *Webster's New Collegiate Dictionary*, 11th ed., s.v. "saturnalia."

9. *Webster's*, s.v. "Yule."

10. Quoted by Kathleen Stokker, *Keeping Christmas: Yuletide Traditions in Norway and the New Land* (St. Paul: Minnesota Historical Society Press, 2000), 7.

11. Stokker, *Keeping Christmas*, 6. I borrow much of the information and several phrases in these paragraphs from Stokker.

12. E. O. James, *Seasonal Feasts and Festivals* (New York: Barnes and Noble, 1961), 292.

TWO **CHRISTMAS COMES LATE**

1. Origen, *Homilies on Leviticus 1–16*, trans. Gary Wayne Barkley (Washington, DC: Catholic University of America Press, 1990), 156–57; Origen, "Commentary on Matthew," in *Ante-Nicene Fathers*, vol. 9, ed. Allan Menzies (Peabody, MA: Hendrickson Publishers, 1994), 428–29. My source for all biblical quotations is the New Revised Standard Version.

2. The only reference by Paul to Jesus' birth is that "God sent his Son, born of a woman" (Galatians 4:4), which does not really tell a nativity story. However, it must be acknowledged that Paul's letters in general do not focus on providing narratives of Jesus' life and teachings; they concentrate more on theology and on advice to early Christian churches.

3. For the general reader, Joseph F. Kelly provides more details about the matter of dates and some of the other topics discussed in this chapter. See esp. chap. 3 in *The Origins of Christmas* (Collegeville, MN: Liturgical Press, 2004). For a very detailed discussion by a noted biblical scholar, see Raymond E. Brown, *The Birth of the Messiah*, rev. ed. (1977; New York: Doubleday, 1993), 166–67 and throughout.

4. Roland H. Bainton, "The Origins of Epiphany," in *Studies in Early Christianity: A Collection of Scholarly Essays*, vol. 15, ed. Everett Ferguson (New York: Garland, 1993), 22; originally printed in *Journal of Biblical Literature*, 1923.

5. Thomas J. Talley, *The Origins of the Liturgical Year*, 2nd ed. (Collegeville, MN: Liturgical Press, 1991), 103–21.

6. Penne L. Restad, *Christmas in America: A History* (New York: Oxford University Press, 1995), 4.

7. Susan K. Roll, *Toward the Origins of Christmas* (Kampen, Netherlands: Kok Pharos Publishing House, 1995), 83–86.

8. Clement A. Miles, *Christmas Customs and Traditions: Their History and Significance* (New York: Dover Publications, 1976), 167–71, 168.

9. Talley, *Origins of the Liturgical Year*, 100.

10. Stephen Nissenbaum, *The Battle for Christmas* (New York: Alfred A. Knopf, 1996), 7–8.

11. Stephanie Coontz, *The Way We Never Were: American Families and the Nostalgia Trap* (New York: Random House, 1994).

12. Kelly, *Origins of Christmas,* 34–35, 40.

13. Robert J. Miller, *Born Divine: The Births of Jesus and Other Sons of God* (Santa Rosa, CA: Polebridge Press, 2003), 267.

14. Paul Barnett, *Is the New Testament Reliable?* 2nd ed. (Downers Grove, IL: InterVarsity Press, 2003), 103–4, 165.

15. Miller, *Born Divine,* 175–77.

16. Brown, *Birth of the Messiah,* 36–37.

THREE CHRISTMAS IS LIKE A SNOWBALL

1. Bertram Colgrave and R. A. B. Mynors, eds., *Bede's Ecclesiastical History of the English People* (Oxford: Clarendon Press, 1969), 107, 109.

2. The centuries listed here do not necessarily reflect the very first Christian contacts in a region but rather the date of Christianity's more substantial presence there.

3. Tanya Gulevich, *Encyclopedia of Christmas* (Detroit: Omnigraphics, 2000), 143.

4. Quoted in Clement A. Miles, *Christmas Customs and Traditions: Their History and Significance* (New York: Dover Publications, 1976), 265.

5. Karal Ann Marling, *Merry Christmas! Celebrating America's Greatest Holiday* (Cambridge, MA: Harvard University Press, 2000), 173–74.

6. Gerry Bowler, *The World Encyclopedia of Christmas* (Toronto: McClelland and Stewart, 2000), 120.

7. See www.aboutflowers.com (accessed August 14, 2006).

8. Michael Patrick Hearn, introduction to *The Annotated Christmas Carol: A Christmas Carol in Prose,* by Charles Dickens (New York: W. W. Norton, 2004), xv.

9. Hearn, introduction.

10. Tom Flynn, *The Trouble with Christmas* (Buffalo, NY: Prometheus Books, 1993), 88.

11. J. M. Golby and A. W. Purdue, *The Making of the Modern Christmas* (Athens: University of Georgia Press, 1986), 36, 40, 44.

12. William Bradford, *Of Plymouth Plantation, 1620–1647,* ed. William T. Davis (New York: Alfred A. Knopf, 1952), 97.

13. Quoted by Stephen Nissenbaum, *The Battle for Christmas* (New York: Alfred A. Knopf, 1996), 14.

14. Quoted by Robert Doares, "Colonial Church Christmases," *Colonial Williamsburg* (Christmas 2005): 29.

15. Golby and Purdue, *Making of the Modern Christmas*, 35.

16. Flynn, *Trouble with Christmas*, 92–93.

17. James H. Barnett, *The American Christmas: A Study in National Culture* (New York: Macmillan, 1954), 19–21.

18. Barnett, *American Christmas*, 16.

19. Barnett, *American Christmas*, 14.

20. Marling, *Merry Christmas!* 137.

21. Marling, *Merry Christmas!* 132, 151–53.

22. Stanley Weintraub, *Albert: Uncrowned King* (London: John Murray, 1997), 114.

23. Marling, *Merry Christmas!* 161.

24. Asa Briggs, *The Age of Improvement, 1783–1867* (London: Longmans, 1959), 447.

25. Flynn, *Trouble with Christmas*, 105.

FOUR FROM SAINT NICHOLAS TO SANTA CLAUS

1. *Catholic Encyclopedia Online* s.v. "St. Nicholas of Myra" (by Michael Ott), www.newadvent.org/cathen/11063b.htm (accessed July 20. 2006).

2. These legends can be found in almost any book about Saint Nicholas. For examples, see the books by the following authors in the bibliography at the end of this volume: Count, Ebon, Flynn, Jones, and Wheeler and Rosenthal.

3. Tom Flynn, *The Trouble with Christmas* (Buffalo, NY: Prometheus Books, 1993), 79; Joe Wheeler and Jim Rosenthal, *St. Nicholas: A Closer Look at Christmas* (Nashville, TN: Thomas Nelson, 2005), 51; Earl W. Count, *4000 Years of Christmas: A Gift from the Ages*, rev. Alice Lawson Count (Berkeley: Ulysses Press, 1997), 66.

4. Count, *4000 Years*, 67.

5. Charles W. Jones, *Saint Nicholas of Myra, Bari, and Manhattan: Biography of a Legend* (Chicago: University of Chicago Press, 1978), 86.

6. Wheeler and Rosenthal, *St. Nicholas*, 79–96.

7. Wheeler and Rosenthal, *St. Nicholas*, 145.

8. Quoted by Jones, *Nicholas of Myra*, 341.

9. Stephen Nissenbaum, *The Battle for Christmas* (New York: Alfred A. Knopf, 1996), 64; Charles Nieder, ed., introduction to *The Complete Tales of Washington Irving* (Garden City, NY: International Collectors Library, 1975), xii.

10. Washington Irving, *Knickerbocker's History of New York* (New York: P. F. Collier and Son, 1904), 71, 93. In case it is not obvious, the phrase "laying his finger aside of his nose" later appeared in "A Visit from St. Nicholas," better known as "The Night Before Christmas," attributed to Clement Moore. The later poem also echoes other aspects of this brief passage from Irving. Irving made revisions to his *History*, so quotations may vary slightly. In this edition, "a very significant look" has been changed to "a very significant wink."

11. Jones, *Nicholas of Myra*, 345, 330.

12. Jones, *Nicholas of Myra*, 344.

13. Tristam Potter Coffin, *The Illustrated Book of Christmas Folklore* (New York: Seabury Press, 1973), 69–71; Don Foster, *Author Unknown: On the Trail of Anonymous* (New York: Henry Holt, 2000), chap. 6; Stephen Nissenbaum, "There Arose Such a Clatter; Who Really Wrote 'The Night Before Christmas'? (And Why Does It Matter?)," *Common-place: The Interactive Journal of Early American Life* 1, no. 2 (January 2001), www.common-place.org.

14. Tanya Gulevich, *Encyclopedia of Christmas* (Detroit: Omnigraphics, 2000), 492.

15. Nissenbaum, *Battle for Christmas*, 73.

16. Gerry Bowler, *The World Encyclopedia of Christmas* (Toronto: McClelland and Stewart, 2000), 252.

17. Editorial, *New York Sun*, September 21, 1897.

18. Editorial, *New York Times*, November 27, 1927.

19. Barbara Fahs Charles and J. R. Taylor, *Dream of Santa: Haddon Sundblom's Advertising Paintings for Christmas, 1931–1964* (New York: Grammercy Books, 1992), 15.

20. Charles and Taylor, *Dream of Santa*, 16.

21. Gerry Bowler, *Santa Claus: A Biography* (Toronto: McClelland and Stewart, 2005), 123, 124.

22. Nissenbaum, *Battle for Christmas*, 65.

FIVE **AND THEN THERE WAS MONEY**

1. W. D. Howells, "Christmas Every Day," in *The Saint Nicholas Anthology*, ed. Henry Steele Commager (New York: Crown Publishers, 1975), 521.

2. Charles Dickens, *The Annotated Christmas Carol*, ed. Michael Patrick Hearn (New York: W. W. Norton, 2004), 26; Leigh Eric Schmidt, *Consumer Rites: The Buying and Selling of American Holidays* (Princeton: Princeton University Press, 1995), 32.

3. William B. Waits, *The Modern Christmas in America: A Cultural History of Gift Giving* (New York: New York University Press, 1994), 3.

4. *New York Times*, December 24, 1880, quoted by Schmidt, *Consumer Rites*, 183.

5. *Sunday School Times*, December 7, 1912, quoted by Schmidt, *Consumer Rites*, 188.

6. Quoted by Waits, *Modern Christmas*, 71.

7. Tanya Gulevich, *Encyclopedia of Christmas* (Detroit: Omnigraphics, 2000), 105; U.S. Postal Service, www.usps.com/communications/news/press/welcome.htm (accessed August 14, 2006).

8. Penne L. Restad, *Christmas in America: A History* (New York: Oxford University Press, 1995), 63.

9. U.S. Census Bureau, Facts for Features, "The Holiday Season," December 19, 2005, www.census.gov (accessed August 30, 2006).

10. All of this information about electric lights comes from Karal Ann Marling, *Merry Christmas! Celebrating America's Greatest Holiday* (Cambridge, MA: Harvard University Press, 2000), 56.

11. Restad, *Christmas in America*, 128.

12. Marling, *Merry Christmas!* 15.

13. *Gifts and Decorative Accessories* (April 1997): 134, cited in Marling, *Merry Christmas!* 1; Gulevich, *Encyclopedia*, 147.

14. Marling, *Merry Christmas!* 32–33.

15. The statistics in the last two paragraphs are from three sources, gathered in turn from a variety of other sources: Gulevich, *Encyclopedia*, 147, 149; the Web site www.newdream.org (accessed July 20, 2006); and "Americans More Generous at Christmas than Europeans," (*Reuters* November 27, 1998).

16. For an account of this story, plus supporting documents, see the FDR Library online at www.fdrlibrary.marist.edu/thanksg.html.

17. Gerry Bowler, *The World Encyclopedia of Christmas* (Toronto: McClelland and Stewart, 2000), 194.

18. Jody Rosen, *White Christmas: The Story of an American Song* (New York: Scribner, 2002), 5–6.

19. The quoted phrase is from James R. Oestreich's review of Rosen's book in the *New York Times*, also published in the *Minneapolis Star Tribune* (December 22, 2002); Rosen, *White Christmas*, 13.

20. "Christmas Pictures," *Moving Picture World*, 18:5 (1913), 1390.

21. Frank Thompson, *Great Christmas Movies* (Dallas: Taylor Publishing, 1998), 141.

six WRESTLING WITH CHRISTMAS

1. Rodney Clapp, *Border Crossings: Christian Trespasses on Popular Culture and Public Affairs* (Grand Rapids, MI: Brazos Press, Baker Book House), 81.

2. Earl W. Count, *4000 Years of Christmas: A Gift from the Ages,* rev. Alice Lawson Count (Berkeley: Ulysses Press, 1997), 98–99.

3. Bill McKibben, *Hundred Dollar Holiday: The Case for a More Joyful Christmas* (New York: Simon and Schuster, 1998), 12.

4. McKibben, *Hundred Dollar Holiday,* 73.

5. Jo Robinson and Jean Coppock Staeheli, *Unplug the Christmas Machine: A Complete Guide to Putting Love and Joy Back into the Season* (New York: William Morrow, 1991), chap. 4.

6. Robinson and Staeheli, *Unplug,* 13.

7. McKibben, *Hundred Dollar Holiday,* 50. In addition to the books by McKibben and by Robinson and Staeheli, one other volume on the same subject is Alice Chapin, *A Simple Christmas* (Scottdale, PA: Herald Press, 1998). Two similarly focused organizations are the Center for the New American Dream (www.newdream.org) and Alternatives for Simple Living, which publishes an annual resource booklet called *Whose Birthday Is It Anyway?* (www.simpleliving.org); and workshop materials to supplement *Unplug.*

8. Tom Flynn, *The Trouble with Christmas* (Buffalo, NY: Prometheus Books, 1993), chaps. 11–13.

9. Lawrence A. Hoffman, "On Being a Jew at Christmas," *Cross Currents* 42, no. 3 (Fall 1992): 363, 358.

10. Quoted by Flynn, *Trouble with Christms,* 163–64.

AN ANNOTATED BIBLIOGRAPHY

Barnett, James H. *The American Christmas: A Study in National Culture*. New York: Macmillan, 1954. xi + 167 pp. Notes, bibliography, and index.

> When Barnett, a University of Connecticut sociologist, wrote this book, he called it "a pioneer effort in the sociological study of American holidays." Quite a few good books have appeared since then, but Barnett's classic early work shows up repeatedly in other scholars' notes and bibliographies.

Barnett, Paul. *Is the New Testament Reliable?* 2nd ed. Downers Grove, IL: Inter-Varsity Press, 2003. 197 pp. Notes and index, no bibliography.

> In this book's tenth chapter, "The Birth of Jesus," Barnett argues that the birth narratives in Matthew and Luke are historically reliable, along with the rest of the New Testament. Barnett was the Anglican bishop of North Sydney, Australia, and has taught in Vancouver and in Australia. To compare this view with other biblical scholarship, also see Brown, Horsley, Miller, and Spong.

Bowler, Gerry. *The World Encyclopedia of Christmas*. Toronto: McClelland and Stewart, 2000. 257 pp. No notes, bibliography, or index.

> Bowler teaches at the University of Manitoba and has published in the fields of history and popular culture. Unlike many popularly written but uncritical collections of Christmas

information, this is a well-researched reference work with over 1,000 short entries. For the other good Christmas encyclopedia, see Gulevich.

Brown, Raymond E. *The Birth of the Messiah: A Commentary on the Infancy Narratives in the Gospels of Matthew and Luke.* New York: Doubleday, 1993. 752 pp. Extensive notes, bibliography, and index.

> The late Raymond Brown, a Catholic, taught biblical studies at Union Theological Seminary in New York City and was widely regarded as a "dean of New Testament scholars." Biblical scholar Robert Miller says this careful, detailed academic work on the gospel narratives of Jesus' birth is "unparalleled both in its scope and in its depth." See also works by other biblical scholars, Barnett, Horsley, Miller, and Spong, in this bibliography.

Coffin, Tristam Potter. *The Illustrated Book of Christmas Folklore.* New York: Seabury Press, 1973. 145 pp. Index, but no notes or bibliography.

> Coffin was a professor of English and folklore at the University of Pennsylvania, and this is an interesting narrative of Christmas folklore. Quite a few of its claims might be revised or supplemented by more recent scholarship.

Connelly, Mark. *Christmas: A Social History.* New York: I. B. Taurus, 1999. 256 pp. Notes, bibliography, and index.

> The book's title does not make it clear, but this volume focuses specifically on the development of Christmas in England from 1780 to 1952. Connelly teaches at the University of Kent at Canterbury, specializing in cultural, social, and film history, and his book includes topical chapters on how Christmas was expressed through music, film, and radio. Overall, however, Connelly also has a larger theme. He argues that recent scholarship about Christmas has overemphasized the idea that Christmas died in England in the late 1700s and was invented anew in the 1800s by Dickens and others. Connelly agrees that Christmas flourished in the 1800s, but he emphasizes continuities, saying that the Victorian Christmas was not a total invention out of nothing. Thus, this is an academic book with a thesis, but it also has many aspects that would interest the general reader, especially for those who are interested in England.

Count, Earl W. *4000 Years of Christmas: A Gift From the Ages.* Rev. Alice Lawson Count. Berkeley: Ulysses Press, 1997. 108 pp. No notes, bibliography, or index.

> In this little book, Earl Count, an Episcopal priest with anthropological background, includes the pre-Christian origins of Christmas (as the time span in the title suggests). First published in 1948, the work has been revised by his widow.

deChant, Dell. *The Sacred Santa: Religious Dimensions of Consumer Culture.* Cleveland: Pilgrim Press, 2002. 224 pp. Notes, index, no bibliography.

To deChant, who teaches in the Department of Religious Studies at the University of South Florida, consumerism is not a secular challenge to Christianity but a religion in its own right, giving meaning to people, and the Sacred Santa is the icon of this religion. deChant studies and describes it, in a somewhat neutral way, as he would study any other religion.

Ebon, Martin. *Saint Nicholas: Life and Legend*. New York: Harper and Row, 1975. 119 pp. Bibliography, no notes or index.

> Throughout Ebon's long career in publishing, journalism, and public relations, he was the author, editor, or translator of more than fifty nonfiction books on a dizzying array of subjects, especially parapsychology, Soviet affairs, and religion. He based his work on serious, balanced research, and one result is this brief survey of information about Saint Nicholas, from his beginnings to recent years.

Flynn, Tom. *The Trouble with Christmas*. Buffalo, NY: Prometheus Books, 1993. 244 pp. Notes, no bibliography or index.

> In this book Flynn gives a brief account of his shift from a Catholic upbringing to atheism, and of his objections to what he sees as the oppressive, dominant role of Christmas in American culture. The work has two parts: a competent history of the development of Christmas, told through Flynn's critical lens, and a discussion of the struggle various non-Christians have with the holiday.

Golby, J. M., and A. W. Purdue. *The Making of the Modern Christmas*. Athens: University of Georgia Press, 1986. 144 pp. Index, no notes or bibliography.

> Golby and Purdue teach history in England, and they argue that the modern Christmas in England and America is mainly a product of the Victorian era and more recent developments. Their view is that older aspects of Christmas were suppressed by the Puritans, and when Victorians brought Christmas back it was an "invented tradition," a new creation built on nostalgia so that it seemed old. Although the book is written for general readers, with interesting information and with illustrations on almost every page, its overall perspective also generates discussion among scholars, both pro and con.

Gulevich, Tanya. *Encyclopedia of Christmas*. Detroit: Omnigraphics, 2000. 730 pp. Bibliography for every encyclopedia entry, and an extensive index for the book overall. No notes.

> Gulevich holds a PhD in cultural anthropology from the University of Michigan, and she wrote this encyclopedia specifically as a reference work for general readers, with an advisory board of librarians as consultants. It is well researched, reliable, refers to other sources, and is now available in paperback. For the other good Christmas encyclopedia, see Bowler.

Horsley, Richard A. *The Liberation of Christmas: The Infancy Narratives in Social Context.* New York: Crossroad, 1989. 201 pp. Notes and index, no bibliography.

> Horsley, a religious studies professor at the University of Massachusetts, Boston, argues that standard discussions about whether the biblical birth narratives of Jesus are historical or symbolic ignore the stories' social context: the tyranny and repression by Caesar and Herod, and the roles of peasants, shepherds, and women as the people who received Jesus. In his view these are narratives of liberation, with strong social implications for politics and world affairs today. The writing style is both academic and passionate. To compare this view with other biblical scholarship, also see Barnett, Brown, Miller, and Spong.

Horsley, Richard, and James Tracy, eds. *Christmas Unwrapped: Consumerism, Christ, and Culture.* Harrisburg, PA: Trinity Press International, 2001. 234 pp. Notes, index, no bibliography.

> This collection of academic essays about Christmas focuses on the "religion of consumer capitalism." Its various authors believe that Nissenbaum's *Battle for Christmas* (also included in this bibliography) deserves more attention than it has been given, and they seek "to actively build upon his catalyzing work." See my comments on academic essays in notes for the other collection (Miller, *Unwrapping Christmas*).

Jones, Charles W. *Saint Nicholas of Myra, Bari, and Manhattan: Biography of a Legend.* Chicago: University of Chicago Press, 1978. 558 pp. Extensive notes, bibliography, and index.

> Jones, a medievalist and a professor emeritus at the University of California, Berkeley, has written the most substantial academic consideration of Saint Nicholas in English in the last few decades. Based on extensive primary research, the book revises some previously accepted historical claims.

Kelly, Joseph F. *The Origins of Christmas.* Collegeville, MN: Liturgical Press, 2004. 145 pp. Bibliography, no notes or index.

> Kelly, a professor of religious studies at John Carroll University, discusses the origins of Christmas until the sixth century. Like Roll and Talley, Kelly is Catholic, which may account for their common interest in liturgies. Kelly's book is a brief and readable volume intended for a general audience (unlike Roll's and Talley's dense academic works).

Marling, Karal Ann. *Merry Christmas! Celebrating America's Greatest Holiday.* Cambridge, MA: Harvard University Press, 2000. 442 pp. Notes and index, no bibliography.

> Marling is a professor of art history at the University of Minnesota with a strong interest in popular culture (her other works range from Elvis to Disney to state fairs). This book

about the American Christmas takes up what scholars call "material culture," the background and meanings of various "things" such as wrapping paper, department store displays, and Coca-Cola Santa collectibles. General readers will like her chatty style.

McKibben, Bill. *Hundred Dollar Holiday: The Case for a More Joyful Christmas.* New York: Simon and Schuster, 1998. 95 pp. No notes, bibliography, or index.

> This charming and tiny little book is an advocacy for a simpler and more joyous Christmas, written by a former staff writer for the *New Yorker* who helped lead programs on this subject among rural upstate New York churches. It fits well with Robinson and Staeheli's *Unplug the Christmas Machine,* also included in this bibliography.

Miles, Clement A. *Christmas Customs and Traditions: Their History and Significance.* New York: Dover Publications, 1976. First published as *Christmas in Ritual and Tradition: Christian and Pagan* (London, 1912). 400 pp. Notes, index, no bibliography.

> This is a very old volume, available in reprint editions, and Stephen Nissenbaum says it remains "the best account of the non-Christian origins of Christmas rituals." Indeed, almost all of the many books on the history of Christmas quote Miles, which indicates a lack of recent research on the various traditions that preceded and influenced Christmas.

Miller, David, ed. *Unwrapping Christmas.* Oxford: Clarendon Press, 1993. 239 pp. Notes, index, bibliography with each essay.

> This is one of two collections of academic essays I have included in this bibliography, each essay written by a different author; the counterpart to *Unwrapping Christmas* is *Christmas Unwrapped.* Original! As in most collections like this, there are strong essays and very weak ones, with different levels of jargon, about very miscellaneous topics. If you are a general reader, this book probably will not interest you (academic readers explore volumes like this for interesting nuggets). For the other collection of essays, see Horsley and Tracy.

Miller, Robert J. *Born Divine: The Births of Jesus and Other Sons of God.* Santa Rosa, CA: Polebridge Press, 2003. 337 pp. Texts of documents, bibliography, and index; no notes.

> Miller is a biblical scholar who teaches at Juniata College and has written about the Jesus Seminar, a controversial academic project to determine which parts of the Christian gospels are historical. In *Born Divine* Miller analyzes the birth narratives of Jesus and of other Hebrew, Greek, and Roman figures who also were believed to be sons of God. The work is fairly understandable for a general audience and includes English translations of some documents on these alternate divine births. Miller concludes that the virgin birth narratives of Jesus are symbolic, not literal history. To compare this view with other biblical scholarship, also see Barnett, Brown, Horsley, and Spong in this bibliography.

Nissenbaum, Stephen. *The Battle for Christmas.* New York: Alfred A. Knopf, 1996. 381 pp. Extensive notes, index, no bibliography.

> The book's long subtitle describes its subject, *A Social and Cultural History of Christmas that Shows How It Was Transformed from an Unruly Carnival into the Quintessential American Family Holiday.* A superb, well-written, insightful work by a history professor at the University of Massachusetts, Amherst, it emphasizes three themes, in connection with larger historical developments: the unrestrained "carnival" aspects of the early American Christmas, the commercialization of the holiday as part of a wider consumer culture, and what the development of a family-centered holiday revealed about child rearing and the shape of the American family. Nissenbaum based his account on more primary research than most Christmas books.

Restad, Penne L. *Christmas in America: A History.* New York: Oxford University Press, 1995. 209 pp. Extensive notes, index, no bibliography.

> Restad teaches American history at the University of Texas at Austin. As the title of this book indicates, this history starts in the American colonies and gives little attention to pre-American roots. It is a fine scholarly history, readable for the general public, with many details.

Robinson, Jo, and Jean Coppock Staeheli. *Unplug the Christmas Machine: A Complete Guide to Putting Love and Joy Back into the Season.* New York: William Morrow, 1991. 207 pp. Index, no notes or bibliography.

> For those who struggle with the commercialization and hectic pace of the Christmas season, this book has become a classic guide. It provides tools for people to discern their own priorities—for a more religious focus, perhaps, or ways to reduce stress—and then make practical decisions. This book is against the Christmas *machine,* not the holiday itself.

Roll, Susan K. *Toward the Origins of Christmas.* Kampen, Netherlands: Kok Pharos Publishing House, 1995. 296 pp. Notes, bibliography, and index.

> Roll, who teaches liturgy, sacraments, and theology at Christ the King Seminary, Buffalo, New York, surveys the evidence and academic theories about the beginnings of Christmas in the first few centuries. If you want specific information about documents and scholars, this is the best recent English-language source: a technical and detailed academic work. Its publication in the Netherlands means that it is not easy to find, most likely in graduate libraries. Also see the books by Talley and Kelly.

Schmidt, Leigh Eric. *Consumer Rites: The Buying and Selling of American Holidays.* Princeton: Princeton University Press, 1995. 363 pp. Extensive notes, index, no bibliography.

Schmidt, a historian of American religion who teaches at Princeton, examines "the interweaving of commerce and the sacred in American holidays," with a focus on Valentine's Day, Christmas, Easter, and Mother's Day. One resource for this book was the archives of Hallmark cards.

Spong, John Shelby. *Born of a Woman: A Bishop Rethinks the Birth of Jesus.* New York: HarperSanFrancisco, 1992. 245 pp. Notes, bibliography, and index.

Spong is an Episcopal bishop who has published several books against Christian fundamentalism and biblical literalism. Rejecting the "literalized symbol" of Mary's virginity, he claims it has been used to legitimize women's second-class status in Western history and argues that a greater emphasis on Mary's humanity is a more empowering image for experiencing God in human history. To compare Spong's view with other biblical scholarship, see Barnett, Brown, Horsley, and Miller in this bibliography.

Stokker, Kathleen. *Keeping Christmas: Yuletide Traditions in Norway and the New Land.* St. Paul: Minnesota Historical Society Press, 2000. 355 pp. Notes, bibliography, and index.

Stokker, a professor of Norwegian at Luther College in Decorah, Iowa, describes ancient Norwegian traditions, the mingling of customs when Norwegian settlers reached the United States, and ongoing developments on both sides of the ocean. Her well-researched book includes first-person accounts, pictures, and even recipes; it should appeal to general readers.

Talley, Thomas J. *The Origins of the Liturgical Year.* 2nd ed. Collegeville, MN: Liturgical Press, 1991. 255 pp. Notes, bibliography, and index.

Talley, a professor of liturgics at the General Theological Seminary in New York and formerly at Notre Dame, discusses academic debates about the beginnings of Epiphany and Christmas, their dates, and whether they are linked with pre-Christian observances. Roll's book on the same subject is more recent and more completely focused on Christmas; also technical and detailed, Talley's book is about the whole liturgical year, and his section on Epiphany and Christmas is recognized for discrediting some widely accepted theories about Epiphany. Also see books by Roll and Kelly.

Waits, William B. *The Modern Christmas in America: A Cultural History of Gift Giving.* New York: New York University Press, 1994. 267 pp. Extensive notes, index, no bibliography.

Waits studies American society through its Christmas gift giving. Using the articles and advertisements of mass market magazines, he focuses on practices since 1880, when manufactured gifts began to replace homemade ones. Waits looks at social structures and dynamics among married couples, parents and children, at work and in other social relationships. Based on his graduate work in anthropology and history, the doctoral dissertation was revised for publication and includes illustrations from popular magazines.

Walsh, Joseph J. *Were They Wise Men or Kings?: The Book of Christmas Questions.* Louisville: Westminster John Knox Press, 2001. 127 pp. Bibliography, no notes or index.

> This attractive little book has chapters about two pages long, each in answer to a question general readers might ask about Christmas. It is well informed by scholarship and written in a clear, informal style. Walsh teaches classics and history at Loyola College in Baltimore and leads an annual seminar about Christmas.

Wheeler, Joe, and Jim Rosenthal. *St. Nicholas: A Closer Look at Christmas.* Nashville, TN: Thomas Nelson, 2005. 278 pp. Notes, bibliography, no index.

> Both Wheeler and Rosenthal are fans of St. Nicholas, and Rosenthal founded the St. Nicholas Society UK/USA. This is an appealing coffee-table book, with full-color photographs, antique cards, and illustrations of St. Nicholas on almost every page, drawn from Rosenthal's personal collection. It is full of information and stories but, unfortunately, the illustrations on most pages do not correlate with the text.

INDEX

Page numbers in italics refer to illustrations.

Designer: Claudia Smelser
Text: 10.5/14 Baskerville
Display: Copperplate Gothic
Compositor: BookComp
Indexer: Marcia Carlson
Printer and Binder: Thomson-Shore, Inc.